CAMBRIDGE LIBRARY COLLECTION

Books of enduring scholarly value

Printing and Publishing History

The interface between authors and their readers is a fascinating subject in its own right, revealing a great deal about social attitudes, technological progress, aesthetic values, fashionable interests, political positions, economic constraints, and individual personalities. This part of the Cambridge Library Collection reissues classic studies in the area of printing and publishing history that shed light on developments in typography and book design, printing and binding, the rise and fall of publishing houses and periodicals, and the roles of authors and illustrators. It documents the ebb and flow of the book trade supplying a wide range of customers with products from almanacs to novels, bibles to erotica, and poetry to statistics.

Exhibition and Market of Machinery, Implements and Material Used by Printers, Stationers, Papermakers and Kindred Trades

First published in 1880, this is a complete catalogue of the traders and products that featured in an exhibition at London's Agricultural Hall, 5–17 July 1880. The focus of the exhibition was printing, stationery, papermaking and related trades, and around 200 organisations participated, displaying items such as printing appliances, papermaking machinery, stationery materials, packaging, and precision instruments. The catalogue's editor, journalist Lucien Wolf (1857–1930), prefaces it with an informative overview of trade exhibitions, examining their history and future, and their role in bringing together producers, retailers, buyers, wholesalers and importers to assess competition, compare products and evaluate the state and progress of their trades. The main body of the catalogue contains information on exhibitors and their products, and a range of authentic advertisements. Providing a revealing snapshot of industrial England, this work remains of interest to historians and scholars interested in Victorian trade.

T0304204

Cambridge University Press has long been a pioneer in the reissuing of out-of-print titles from its own backlist, producing digital reprints of books that are still sought after by scholars and students but could not be reprinted economically using traditional technology. The Cambridge Library Collection extends this activity to a wider range of books which are still of importance to researchers and professionals, either for the source material they contain, or as landmarks in the history of their academic discipline.

Drawing from the world-renowned collections in the Cambridge University Library and other partner libraries, and guided by the advice of experts in each subject area, Cambridge University Press is using state-of-the-art scanning machines in its own Printing House to capture the content of each book selected for inclusion. The files are processed to give a consistently clear, crisp image, and the books finished to the high quality standard for which the Press is recognised around the world. The latest print-on-demand technology ensures that the books will remain available indefinitely, and that orders for single or multiple copies can quickly be supplied.

The Cambridge Library Collection brings back to life books of enduring scholarly value (including out-of-copyright works originally issued by other publishers) across a wide range of disciplines in the humanities and social sciences and in science and technology.

Exhibition and Market of Machinery, Implements and Material Used by Printers, Stationers, Papermakers and Kindred Trades

Official Catalogue of Exhibits

Lucien Wolf

CAMBRIDGE
UNIVERSITY PRESS

CAMBRIDGE UNIVERSITY PRESS

Cambridge, New York, Melbourne, Madrid, Cape Town,
Singapore, São Paolo, Delhi, Mexico City

Published in the United States of America by Cambridge University Press, New York

www.cambridge.org
Information on this title: www.cambridge.org/9781108057387

© in this compilation Cambridge University Press 2013

This edition first published 1880
This digitally printed version 2013

ISBN 978-1-108-05738-7 Paperback

ENTERED AT STATIONERS' HALL.

PRINTING, STATIONERY, PAPER MAKING & KINDRED TRADES, EXHIBITION & MARKET, CATALOGUE.

AGRICULTURAL HALL, LONDON.

July 5th to July 17th 1880

SIXPENCE.

THE CROWN STEAM PRINTING CO. LITHOGRAPHERS, ETC., CROWN COURT, MILTON ST., LONDON, E.C.

EXHIBITION & MARKET

OF

Machinery, Implements & Material

USED BY

PRINTERS, STATIONERS, PAPERMAKERS

AND

KINDRED TRADES.

~~~~~~~~~~~~~~~~~~~~~~~~~~~~~~~~

OFFICIAL

CATALOGUE OF EXHIBITS.

EDITED BY

LUCIEN WOLF,

Author of "Reminiscences of the Paris Exhibition;" Editor of the Officia
Catalogue of the National Exhibition and Market; etc. etc.

LONDON:

PUBLISHED BY ROBERT DALE, AT THE AGRICULTURAL HALL.

1880.

CONTENTS.

Patrons.

THE RT. HON. SIR FRANCIS WYATT TRUSCOTT, LORD MAYOR OF LONDON.

THE RT. HON. E. DWYER-GRAY, M.P., LORD MAYOR OF DUBLIN.

THE RT. HON. THOMAS J. BOYD, LORD PROVOST OF EDINBURGH.

THE RT. HON. WILLIAM COLLINS, LORD PROVOST OF GLASGOW.

DR. CHARLES CAMERON, M.P., PRESIDENT OF THE COMPANY OF STATIONERS OF GLASGOW.

JOHN WALTER, ESQ., M.P.

W. J. INGRAM, ESQ., M.P.

EDWARD LLOYD, ESQ.

MESSRS. WM. & GEO. CLOWES.

MESSRS. SPOTTISWOODE & CO.

MESSRS. EYRE & SPOTTISWOODE.

MESSRS. WATERLOW BROTHERS & LAYTON.

MESSRS. BEMROSE & SONS.

MESSRS. WATERLOW & SONS, LIMITED.

MESSRS. MARCUS WARD & CO.

And under the Especial Patronage and Sanction of the Council of the Printers' Pension, Almshouse, and Orphan Asylum Corporation.

ROBERT DALE,
Seeretary and Manager.

INDEX OF EXHIBITORS.

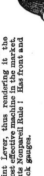

CLASSIFIED GUIDE TO EXHIBITS.

N.B.—In the following list of Exhibits it has been found impossible to give the special characteristics of each special Exhibit, except where it has been tersely made clear in the *name* provided by the Exhibitor himself. To transcribe the lengthier *description* of these specialities here has, of course, been quite out of the question. Where any doubt as to the identity of an Exhibit exists, it may be quickly and easily resolved by inspecting the Exhibit itself, which will readily be found if this guide be followed.

I.—PRINTING MACHINERY AND APPLIANCES.

EXHIBIT.	EXHIBITOR.	Row.	No. of Space.
" Albion," Genuine, Printing Press ...	Hopkinson & Cope ...	East Side	27
" Alexandria " Hand Printing Press	W. Notting	Bay	7
Anglo-American " Arab " Platen Printing Machine	J. Wade	No. 27	80
Anglo-French Lithographic Machine, Double Demy	Conisbee & Son ...	No. 33	154
" Arab " Platen Printing Machine, Anglo-American	J. Wade	No. 27	80
Atlas Foolscap Folio Treadle Platen Printing Machine	Conisbee & Son ...	No. 33	154
" Autographic " Printing Press ...	Waterlow & Sons, Ltd	North Side	34
" Bacon's " Patent Multiple Colour Printing Apparatus	T. Middleton & Co.	Bay	12
Black Leading Machine, Electrotype	W. & G. Clowes ...	North Side	33
" Blocklet " Initialer and Numberer Stamp	Patent Printing Surface Co.,	No. 33	152
Boomer Patent Printing Press ...	J. H. Ladd & Co. ...	No. 27	83
Bremner Machine, Crown Folio, Harrild & Sons' New Patent Treadle	J. E. H. Andrew ...	Bay	18
Bremner Machine, Demy, Harrild & Sons'	,,	,,	18

EXHIBIT.	EXHIBITOR.	Row.	No. of Space.
Brissard Patent One Cylinder Ruling Machine	H. Everling ...	Bay	2
Brissard Patent Two Cylinder Ruling Machine	,,	,,	11
"Caxton" Foolscap Folio Platen Printing Machine	Furnival & Co. ...	East Side	26
"City" Improved Printing Machine	F. Ullmer	Bay	21
Colour Printing Apparatus, "Bacon's" Patent Multiple	T. Middleton & Co.	,,	12
Colour Wharfedale Printing Press, Payne's Demy	Hopkinson & Cope ...	East Side	27
"Columbian" Printing Press ...	W. Notting	Bay	7
Compo-Lithographic Apparatus ...	Compo-Lithograph Co.	No. 28	91
Copying Apparatus, "Hektograph"	Fairholme & Co. ...	Bay	23
,, ,, "Multiscript"	,,	,,	23
Copying Presses	B. Sulman	No. 35	188
,, ,, Screw and Portable	S. Mordan & Co. ...	No. 35	189
Copyograph, "Paragon"	Baddeley & Reynolds	No. 25	42
"Crown Albion" Printing Press ...	F. Ullmer	Bay	21
"Crown" Lithographic Machine ...	Newsum, Wood and Dyson.	,,	17
Croxon's "Lightning" Printing Machine.	Fenner & Appleton ...	East Side	25
Cylinder Plate Printing Machine ...	Bradbury, Wilkinson and Co.	Bay	22
Dating Press, Railway Ticket ...	Waterlow & Sons, Limited.	North Side	34
Dating Stamp, "Paragon"	Baddeley & Reynolds	No. 25	42
Deardin & Newsum's Lithographic Machine.	Riddle & Couchman	Bay	20
Demy Folio "Wimbledon" Machine	Conisbee & Son ...	No. 33	154
Design Stamp, Indiarubber	City Rubber Stamp Company.	No. 34	176
Die-Sinking Press	B. Sulman	No. 35	188
Double Demy Anglo-French Litho-graphic Machine.	Conisbee & Son ...	No. 33	154
Double Demy Letter-press Wharfe-dale Printing Machine.	T. Long & Co. ...	North Side	35
Double Double Crown Lithographic Machine.	Newsum, Wood and Dyson.	Bay	17
Draughtsmen's Utensils	Zorn, Bahnson & Co.	No. 36	197
"Durable" Rollers	Durable Printer Roller Company.	No. 30	111
Electrotype Blackleading Machine ...	W. & G. Clowes ...	North Side	33

Exhibit.	Exhibitor.	Row.	No. of Space.
Embossing Presses	B. Sulman	No. 53	188
,, ,, Lever and Screw	Baddeley & Reynolds	No. 25	42
Endorsing Presses	,, ,,	,,	,,
Endorsement Stamps, Indiarubber ...	City Rubber Stamp Company.	No. 34	176
Engraving Machines and Utensils ...	Zorn, Bahnson & Co.	No. 36	197
"Express" Lithographic Machine ...	Furnival & Co. ...	East Side	26
"Galley's Improved Universal" Platen Printing Machine.	J. L. Chapin & Co. ...	Centre of	Gt. Hall
Genuine "Albion" Printing Press ...	Hopkinson & Cope ...	East Side	27
Gold Lettering Machine, Mackay's ...	Field & Tuer... ...	No. 26	70
Gough's Patent Cameo Colour Stamping Press.	J. Richmond & Co. ...	No. 31	124
Gough's Patent Relief Colour Stamping Press.	,, ,, ...	,,	,,
Greenwood & Kritch's Patent "Sun" Platen Printing Machine.	Greenwood & Batley	North Side	31
Handbills, Press for Printing, from rubber dyes.	City Rubber Stamp Co.	No. 34	176
Hand Press, "Alexandria"	W. Notting	Bay	7
Hand Press, Patent "Simplissimus" Self-Inking.	Birmingham Machinists' Co.	,,	10
Harrild & Sons' Crown Folio New Patent Treadle Bremner.	J. E. H. Andrew ...	,,	18
Harrild & Sons' Demy Bremner Machine.	,, ,, ...	,,	,,
"Hektograph" Copying Apparatus...	Fairholme & Co. ...	,,	23
Hickok's No. O.A. Pennsylvanian Ruling Machine.	M'Cormick & Begg ...	North Side	38
Hooker's Type Composing Machine...	W. & G. Clowes ...	,,	33
Hydraulic Presses, 6-in.	J. Richmond & Co. ...	No. 31	124
Illuminating Presses	B. Sulman	No. 35	188
India-rubber Design Stamp	City Rubber Stamp Company.	No. 34	176
,, ,, Endorsement Stamp ...	City Rubber Stamp Company.	,,	,,
,, ,, Initial ,, ...	City Rubber Stamp Company.	,,	,,
,, ,, Monogram ,, ...	City Rubber Stamp Company.	,,	,,
,, ,, Stamps	Baddeley & Reynolds	No. 25	42
,, ,, ,, Pure	B. Sulman	No. 35	188
,, ,, Trade Mark Stamp ...	City Rubber Stamp Company.	No. 34	176

B

Exhibit.	Exhibitor.	Row.	No. of Space.
Initial Stamp, Indiarubber	City Rubber Stamp Company.	No. 34	176
"Invicta" Platen Printing Machine.	Birmingham Machinists' Company.	Bay	10
Lever and Screw Embossing Presses	Baddeley & Reynolds	No. 25	42
,, Presses	B. Sulman	No. 35	188
,, Seal Press	S. Mordan & Co. ...	,,	189
"Lightning" Printing Machine, Croxon's.	Fenner & Appleton ...	East Side	25
Lithographic Machine	G. Mann & Co. ...	North Side	30
,, ,, Crown ...	Newsum, Wood, and Dyson.	Bay	17
,, ,, Deardin & Newsum's.	Riddle & Couchman...	,,	20
,, ,, Demy Folio "Wimbledon.'	Conisbee & Son ...	No. 33	154
,, ,, Double Demy Anglo-French.	,, ,, ...	,,	,,
,, ,, "Express" ...	Furnival & Co. ...	East Side	26
,, ,, Improved Double Double Crown.	Newsum, Wood and Dyson.	Bay	17
Lithographic Stones, Grey and Yellow	Zorn, Bahnson & Co.	No. 36	197
,, Writers' Utensils ...	,, ,, ,,	,,	,,
Mackay's Gold Lettering Machine ...	Field & Tuer... ...	No. 26	70
"Minerva" Platen Printing Machine	H. S. Cropper & Co ...	No. 36	195
"Model," The, Printing Press ...	C. G. Squintani & Co.	Centre of	Gt. Hall
Monogram Doré Stamp	Patent Printing Surface Company.	No. 33	152
,, Stamp, Indiarubber ...	City Rubber Stamp Company.	No. 34	176
"Multiscript" Copying Apparatus ...	Fairholme & Co. ...	Bay	23
"Multum" 3 and 4 Facet Stamps ...	Patent Printing Surface Company.	No. 33	152
Numbering Machine, Type	Waterlow & Sons, Ltd.	North Side	34
Numerators	Baddley & Reynolds	No. 25	42
Official Seal Engraving Presses ...	B. Sulman	No. 35	188
Pads, Stamp	Patent Printing Surface Co.	No. 33	152
"Paragon" Copyograph	Baddeley & Reynolds	No. 25	42
,, Dating Stamps	,,	,,	,,
Payne's Demy Colour Wharfedale Printing Press	Hopkinson & Cope ...	East Side	27
Pencil Stamp	Patent Printing Surface Co.	No. 33	152

EXHIBIT.	EXHIBITOR.	Row.	No. of Space.
Pens and Slides Ruling Machines ...	W. Vickery	No. 32	147
Plates, Stencil..	M. Marx	No. 33	163
Pocket Facet Stamp	Patent Printing Surface Co.	No. 33	152
Polygonal Stamps, Patent	,,	,,	,,
Portable Copying Press	S. Mordan and Co. ...	No. 35	189
Powel's Quadrant Demy Printing Machine	Fairholme and Co. ...	Bay.	23
Press, "Alexandria," Hand Printing	W. Notting	,,	7
Press, Copying	B. Sulman	No. 35	188
,, ,, Screw & Portable	S. Mordan and Co. ...	,,	189
,, Dye-sinking...	B. Sulman	,,	188
,, Embossing	,,	,,	,,
,, ,, Lever	Baddeley & Reynolds	No. 25	42
,, ,, Screw	,, ,,	,,	,,
,, Endorsing	,, ,,	,,	,,
,, Hydraulic 6-in.	J. Richmond and Co.	No. 31	124
,, Illuminating...	B. Sulman	No. 35	188
,, Lever...	,, ...	,,	,,
,, Official Seal Engraving ...	,, ...	,,	,,
,, Railway Ticket Dating ...	Waterlow & Sons, Ltd.	North Side	34
,, Relief Stamping	B. Sulman	No. 35	188
,, Screw	,, ...	,,	,,
,, Screw Seal	S. Mordan and Co. ...	No. 35	189
,, "Simplissimus" Self-Inking Hand.	Birmingham Machinists' Co.	Bay	10
Printing Machine, Anglo-American "Arab" Patent Platen.	J. Wade	No. 27	80
Printing Machine, Croxon's "Lightning."	Fenner and Appleton	East Side	25
,, ,, Cylinder Plate ...	Bradbury, Wilkinson and Co.	Bay	22
,, ,, Demy Improved "Standard."	F. Ullmer	,,	21
,, ,, Demy "Standard."	,,	,,	,,
,, ,, Double Demy Letter Press, Wharfedale.	T. Long and Co. ...	North Side	35
,, ,, Foolscap Folio Atlas Treadle Platen.	W. Conisbee and Son.	No. 33	154
Printing Machine, "Caxton" Foolscap Folio Platen	Furnival & Co. ...	East Side	26
Printing Machine, "Gally's Patent Improved Universal" Platen	J. L. Chapin & Co. ...	Centre of	Gt. Hall

Exhibit.	Exhibitor.	Row.	No. of Space.
I r ntingMachine,Greenwood &Kritch's Patent " Sun " Platen	Greenwood & Batley	North Side	31
Printing Machine, Improved Patent " City "	H. Ingle & Co ...	Bay	23
Printing Machine, "Invictus " Platen	Birmingham Machinists' Co.	,,	10
,, ,, Mark Smith's Patent Flyer or Demy " Reliance "	J. Salmon	,,	4
Printing Machine, " Minerva " Platen	H. S. Cropper & Co....	No. 36	195
,, ,, Powell's Quadrant Demy	Fairholme & Co. ...	Bay	23
Printing Machine, Railway Ticket ...	Waterlow & Sons. Ltd.	North Side	34
,, ,, "Reliance" Wharfedale	Fieldhouse & Elliot ...	,,	36
,, ,, Universal Treadle Platen	Hopkinson & Cope ...	East Side	27
Printing Press, Boomer Patent ...	J. H. Ladd & Co. ...	No. 27	83
,, ,, " Crown Albion " ...	F. Ullmer	Bay	21
,, ,, for Printing Handbills from Rubber Dyes	City Rubber Stamp Co.	No. 34	176
,, ,, Genuine "Albion" ...	Hopkinson & Cope ...	East Side	27
,, ,, H. S. Demy, Treadle Wharfedale	,,	,,	,,
,, ,, Improved " Autographic "	Waterlow & Sons, Ltd.	North Side	34
Printing Press,Improved "Columbian"	W. Notting	Bay	7
,, ,, Payne's Demy Colour Wharfedale	Hopkinson & Cope ...	East Side	27
Printing Press, "The Model " ...	C. G. Squintani & Co.	Centre of	Gt. Hall
Pure Rubber Stamps	B. Sulman	No. 35	188
Railway Ticket Dating Press ...	Waterlow & Sons, Ltd.	North Side	34
,, ,, Printing Machine ...	,,	,,	,,
" Reliance " Demy Printing Machine	J. Salmon	Bay	4
,, Wharfedale ,, ,,	Fieldhouse & Elliot ...	North Side	36
Relief Stamping Presses	B. Sulman	No. 35	188
Rollers	J. B. Cumming ...	No. 32	145
,, " The Durable "	Durable Printer Roller Co., Limited	No. 30	114
,, Lithographic	LanhamRollerCo.,Ltd.	No. 25	55
,, Typographic	,,	,,	,,
,, " Ultimatum " India-rubber	Durable Printer Roller Co., Limited	No. 30	114
Ruling Machine, Brissard Patent One Cylinder	H. Everling	Bay	2

Exhibit.	Exhibitor.	Row.	No. of Space.
Ruling Machine, Brisard Patent Two Cylinder	H. Everling	Bay	2
Ruling Machine, Hickok's Patent No O. A. Pennsylvanian	M'Cormick & Begg ...	North Side	38
Ruling Machine, Pens and Slides ...	W. Vickery	No. 32	147
,, ,, Shaw's Double ...	Fenner & Appleton ...	East Side	25
,, ,, ,, Single Striker	,,	,,	,,
Ruling Machine, Slate	D. Hammond ...	No. 34	177
Screw Copying Press	S. Mordan & Co. ...	No. 35	189
,, Embossing Press	Baddeley & Reynolds	No. 25	42
,, Presses	B. Sulman	No. 35	188
,, Seal Press	S. Mordan & Co. ...	,,	189
Seal Engraving Press, Official ...	B. Sulman	,,	188
,, Press, Lever	S. Mordan & Co ...	,,	189
,, ,, Screw	,, ,, ...	,,	,,
Shaw's Double Ruling Machine ...	Fenner & Appleton ...	East Side	25
Shaw's Single Striker Ruling Machine	Fenner & Appleton ...	East Side	25
" Simplissimus " Self-Inking Hand Press	Birmingham Machinists' Company ...	Bay	10
Slate Ruling Machine...	D. Hammond ...	No. 34	177
Slides and Pens Ruling Machine ...	W. Vickery	No. 32	147
Stamping Press, Gough's Patent Cameo Colour.	J. Richmond & Co. ...	No. 31	124
Stamping Press, Gough's Patent Relief Colour	,, ,, ...	,,	,,
Stamp Pads	Patent Printing Surface Co.	No. 33	152
Stamps, " Blocklet " Initialer and Numberer.	,, ,, ,,	,,	,,
,, India-rubber	Baddeley & Reynolds	No. 25	42
,, ,, ,, Design	City Rubber Stamp Co.	No. 34	176
,, ,, ,, Endorsement ...	,, ,, ...	,,	,,
,, ,, ,, Initial	,, ,, ...	,,	,,
,, ,, ,, Monogram ...	,, ,, ...	,,	,,
,, ,, ,, Trade Marks ...	,, ,, ...	,,	,,
,, " Multum,"Three and Four Facet	Patent Printing Surface Co.	No. 33	152
,, " Paragon," Dating	Baddeley & Reynolds..	No. 25	42
,, " Pencil," " Pocket Facet," Monogram, and Doré	Patent Printing Surface Co.	No. 33	152
,, Polygonal	,, ,, ...	,,	,,
,, Pure Rubber	B. Sulman	No. 35	188

Exhibit.	Exhibitor.	Row.	No. of Space.
Stamps, "Universal" Facet and Dater	Patent Printing Surface Co.	No. 33	152
"Standard" Demy Improved Printing Machine.	F. Ullmer	Bay	21
„ „ Printing Machine..	„	„	„
Stencil Plates	M. Marx	No. 33	163
Stereotype Apparatus, Improved ...	Birmingham Machinists' Co.	Bay	10
Stones, Lithographic	Zorn, Bahnson & Co.	No. 36	197
Trade Mark Stamp, India Rubber ...	City Rubber Stamp Co.	No. 34	176
Treadle Bremner Machine, Crown Folio, Harrild & Sons' New Patent	J. E. H. Andrew ...	Bay	18
Treadle Platen Printing Machine, Foolscap Folio, "Atlas".	W. Conisbee & Son ...	No. 33	154
Treadle Platen Printing Machine Foolscap Folio, "Universal"	Hopkinson & Cope ...	East Side	27
Treadle Wharfedale Printing Press, H.S. Demy.	„ „ ...	„	„
"Trypograph," Zuccato's Patent ...	Zuccato & Wolff ...	No. 31	130
Type Composing Machine, Hooker's	W. & G. Clowes ...	North Side	33
Type Numbering Machine	Waterlow and Sons, Limited.	„	34
"Ultimatum" India-rubber Rollers	Durable Printer Roller Company.	No. 30	114
"Universal" Facet & Dater Stamps	Patent Printing Surface Co.	No. 33	152
„ Treadle Platen Printing Machine	Hopkinson & Cope....	East Side	27
Wimbledon Machine, Demy Folio ...	Conisbee & Son. ...	No. 33	154
Wood Engraving, Specimens of ...	Hill and Co.... ...	No. 34	178
Writers' Utensils, Lithographic ...	Zorn, Bahnson & Co.	No. 36	197
Wharfedale Printing Machine, Dbl. Demy Letterpress.	T. Long and Co. ...	North Side	35
Wharfedale Printing Machine, "Reliance."	Fieldhouse and Elliot.	„	36
Wharfedale Printing Press, Payne's Demy Colour.	Hopkinson and Cope.	East Side	27
Zuccato's Patent "Trypograph" ...	Zuccato and Wolff ...	No. 31	130

II.—PAPER MACHINERY.

Exhibit.	Exhibitor.	Row.	No. of Space.
"Advance," The Cutting Machine...	W. Crosland	Bay	14
Anderson's Wire Guide	J. Sturrock & Son ...	No. 30	120
"Ashley," The, Paper Feeder ...	W. H. Bond	Bay	12
Bank Note Moulds	T. J. Marshall & Co....	No. 29	96
Bars and Plates, Cutting, Improved Composition.	Grey & Marten ...	No. 36	203
Bars, Roller	Crookes, Roberts & Co.	No. 30	117
Bearings, Grooved for Hot Cylinders	A. Sheldon	,,	115
Boards, Fence	The Avalon Leather Board Company.	No. 26	62
,, Glasing	The Avalon Leather Board Company.	,,	,,
Bookfolding and Sewing Combination Machine.	Ihlee & Horne ...	Bay	11
Bookfolding Machine, Patent ...	,, ,, ...	,,	,,
Brass Engine Plates	A. Sheldon	No. 30	115
Bruce's Wire Guide	J. Sturrock & Son ...	,,	120
Calender	W. F. Heim	Bay	3
Calender Roll, Finished Chilled English Iron.	Masson and Scott ...	East Side	28
Card Cutter	F. Ullmer	Bay	21
,, The "Elm City" ...	J. L. Chapin and Co..	Centre of	Gt. Hall
Centrifugal Drying Machine ...	Müller, Uhlich & Co.	No. 32	139
Chopper Knives	Crookes, Roberts & Co.	No. 30	117
Chopping Machine, Railway Ticket	Waterlow & Sons, Ltd.	North Side	34
Circular Board Cutter and Tracer, Lhermitte's Improved.	H. Everling	Bay	2
,, Cutters	Crookes Roberts & Co.	No. 30	117
Combined Cutting and Scoring Machine	W. Crosland ...	Bay	14
Composition Cutting Plates & Bars, Improved.	Grey and Marten ...	No. 36	203
Corner Cutting Machine	W. Crosland	Bay	14
Cutter, Card	F. Ullmer	,,	21
Cutters, Circular	Crookes, Roberts & Co.	No. 30	117
,, Envelope	J. Richmond & Co. ...	No. 31	124
,, for Lever Machines	T. Kendell	Bay	1
,, The "Elm City" Card ...	J. L. Chapin & Co. ...	Centre of	Gt. Hall

Exhibit.			Exhibitor.	Row.	No. of Space.
Cutting Machine	...	... ...	G. & W. Bertram ...	North Side	32
,,	Corner ...	...	W. Crosland ...	Bay	14
,,	"Diamond,"	Self-Clamp.	Hazell, Watson and Viney.	,,	1
,,	Envelope...	...	Fenner & Appleton ...	East Side	25
,,	"Express,"	Self-Clamp Guillotine	Furnival and Co. ...	,,	26
,,	Guillotine ...	...	F. Ullmer	Bay	21
,,	,, ...	...	J. Richmond & Co. ...	No. 31	124
,,	Lever Envelope ...		T. Kendell	Bay	1
,,	Millboard ...	...	Fieldhouse & Elliott	North Side	36
,,	Paper	... ...	C. G. Squintani & Co.	Centre of	Gt Hall
,,	for Cutting Watermark Papers.		G. Tidcombe & Son.	Bays	15 & 16
,,	Reay's Patent Envelope.		J. Richmond & Co. ...	No. 31	124
,,	Rotary Millboard...		W. Crosland ...	Bay	14
Cutting and Scoring Machine, Combined.			,,	,,	,,
Cutting Machine	...	... ...	W. F. Heim	,,	3
,,	the "Advance" ...		W. Crosland... ...	,,	14
,,	The "Gem," Paper		J. L. Chapin & Co. ...	Centre of	Gt Hall
,,	Three-side...	...	H. Everling	Bay	2
,,	"Universal," Job & Label.		Furnival & Co. ...	East Side	26
,,	Vertical & Diagonal Paper.		W. Conisbee & Son ...	No. 33	154
,,	"Eclipse" Guillotine.		J. Salmon	,,	4
,,	Undercut Self-clamping.		Lawrence Bros. ...	,,	13
,,	"Victory" Guillotine.		J. Salmon	,,	4
Cutting Plates and Bars, Improved Composition.			Grey and Marten ...	No. 36	203
Damping Machine	...	... ...	A. Annandale ...	East Side.	29
Dandy Roll Carriages, Improved "Universal"			T. J. Marshall & Co...	No. 29	96
,, Rolls ...	...	... ...	,, ,, ...	,,	,,
Destroying Machine, Railway Ticket			Waterlow & Sons, Limited.	North Side	34
Diagonal Paper Cutting Machine, Vertical and			W. Conisbee & Son....	No. 33	154

Exhibit.	Exhibitor.	Row.	No. of Space.
"Diamond" Self-Clamp Cutting Machine.	Hazell, Watson & Viney.	Bay	1
Drying Cylinders, Gland Cock and Knee and Gland for	J. Sturrock & Son ...	No. 30	120
Drying Cylinders, Steam Cock and Knee for	,, ,, ...	,,	,,
Drying Machine, Centrifugal ...	Müller, Uhlich & Co..	No. 32	139
Dry Pressing Machine, Patent Process and Improved.	McCormick & Begg ...	North Side	38
"Eclipse" Guillotine Cutting Machine	J. Salmon	Bay	4
"Elm City," The, Card Cutter ...	J. L. Chapin & Co. ...	Centre of	Gt. Hall
Envelope Cutters	J. Richmond & Co. ...	No. 31	124
,, Cutting Machine	Fenner & Appleton ...	East Side	25
,, ,, ,, Lever ...	T. Kendell	Bay	1
,, ,, ,, Reay's Patent.	J. Richmond & Co. ...	No. 31	124
,, Folding Machine	T. Kendell	Bay	1
,, ,, ,, ...	Fenner & Appleton ...	East Side	25
,, ,, ,, Reay's Patent.	J. Richmond & Co. ...	No. 31	124
,, Gumming Machine... ...	T. Kendell	Bay	1
Engine Plates, Brass	Crookes, Roberts & Co.	No. 30	117
,, ,, ,, ...	A. Sheldon	,,	115
"Express" Self-Clamp Guillotine Cutting Machine.	Furnival & Co. ...	East Side	26
Eyeleting Presses	S. Mordan & Co. ...	No. 35	189
Eyelet Machine	F. Ullmer	Bay	21
Fence Boards	The Avalon Leather Board Co.	No. 26	62
Feeder, The "Ashley" Paper ...	W. H. Bond	Bay	12
Flat Jogging Strainer Frame ...	H. Watson & Son ...	No. 30	121
Folding and Sewing Combination Machine, Book	Ihlee & Horne ...	Bay	11
Folding Machine, Envelope	Fenner & Appleton ...	East Side	25
,, ,, ,, ...	T. Kendell	Bay	1
,, ,, Luggage Label ...	W. Crosland	,,	14
,, ,, Patent Book ...	Ihlee & Horne ...	,,	11
,, ,, Quire	Lawrence Bros. ...	,,	13
,, ,, ,, ...	J. Richmond & Co. ...	No. 31	124
,, ,, Reay's Patent Envelope	,, ...	,,	,,
,, ,, Richmond & Co.'s Quire	J. E. H. Andrew ...	Bay	18

EXHIBIT.	EXHIBITOR.	Row.	No. of Space.
Frame, Flat Jogging Strainer ...	H. Watson & Son ...	No. 30	121
Gearing, Paper Mill	A. Sheldon	No. 30	115
" Gem " The, Paper Cntting Machine	J. L. Chapin & Co. ...	Centre of	Gt. Hall
Gill's Patent Hot Rolling Machine ...	Furnival & Co. ...	East Side	26
Gland Cock and Knee and Gland for Drying Cylinders	J. Sturrock & Son ...	No. 30	120
Glazing Boards	The Avalon Leather Board Co.	No. 26	62
Grooved Bearings for Hot Cylinders	A. Sheldon	No. 30	115
Grooving and Sharpening Machine ...	„	„	115
Guillotine Cutting Machine	J. Richmond & Co. ...	No. 31	124
„ „ „ " Eclipse "	J. Salmon	Bay	4
„ „ „ " Express " Self Clamp	Furnival & Co. ...	East Side	26
„ „ „ 26-in. ...	F. Ullmer	Bay	21
„ „ „ " Victory "	J. Salmon	„	4
Guillotine, Hand	Furnival & Co. ...	East Side	26
Gumming Machine, Envelope ...	T. Kendell	Bay	1
Hand Guillotine	Furnival & Co. ...	East Side	26
Hot Cylinders, Grooved Bearings for	A. Sheldon	No. 30	115
„ Rolling Machine, Gill's Patent	Furnival & Co. ...	East Side	26
Hydraulic Presses	J. Richmond & Co. ...	No. 31	124
Ibotson's Patent Strainer	G. Tidcombe and Son	Bays	15 & 16
Improved Composition Cutting Plates and Bars.	Grey and Marten ...	No. 36	203
Improved Patent Wire Guide ...	J. Sturrock and Son .	No. 30	120
Job and Label Cutting Machine, " Universal."	Furnival and Co.	East Side.	26
Jogging Strainer Frame, Flat ...	H. Watson and Son .	No. 30	121
Knee and Gland and Gland Cock for Drying Cylinders.	J. Sturrock and Son .	„	120
Knee and Steam Cock for Drying Cylinders.	„ „	„	„
Knives, Chopper	Crookes, Roberts & Co.	„	117
„ Millboard	„ „ „	„	„
„ Paper	„ „ „	„	„
Knotter	J. Bertram and Son .	North Side	37
Knotterbottoms	A. Annandale ...	East Side	29
Knotter Plates, Strainer of	G. & W. Bertram ...	North Side	32
Label and Job Cutting Machine, " Universal."	Furnival & Co. ...	East Side	26
„ Luggage Folding Machine ...	W. Crosland	Bay	14

EXHIBIT.	EXHIBITOR.	Row.	No. of Space.
Lever Envelope Cutting Machine ...	T. Kendell	Bay	1
,, Machines, Cutters for	,, ...	,,	,,
Lhermitte's Improved Circular Board Cutter and Tracer.	H. Everling	,,	2
,, ,, Perforating Machine	,, ...	,,	,,
Long Shearing Machine, Railway Ticket.	Waterlow & Sons, Ltd.	North Side	34
Luggage Label Folding Machine ...	W. Crosland	Bay	14
Millboard Cutting Machines	Fieldhouse & Elliot ...	North Side	36
,, ,, ,, Rotary ...	W. Crosland	Bay	14
,, Knives	Crookes, Roberts & Co.	No. 30	117
Mitreing Machine	F. Ullmer	Bay	21
Moulds, Bank Note	T. J. Marshall & Co. ..	Row 29	96
Model of Rag Engine	H. Cooke & Co. ...	No. 30	116
Paging Machine	F. Ullmer	Bay	21
Paper Cutting Machine	C. G. Squintani & Co.	Centre of	Gt. Hall
,, ,, The "Gem"	J. L. Chapin & Co. ...	,,	,,
,, ,, Vertical & Diagonal	W. Conisbee & Son ...	No. 33	154
Paper Feeder, The "Ashley" ...	W. H. Bond	Bay	12
,, Knives	Crookes, Roberts & Co.	No. 30	117
,, Machine Wires	T. J. Marshall & Co. ...	No. 29	96
,, Mill Gearing	A. Sheldon	No. 30	115
Patent Process and Improved Dry Pressing Machine	M'Cormick & Begg ...	North Side	38
Perforating Machine	J. Salmon	Bay	4
,, ,, ...	F. Ullmer	,,	21
,, ,, ...	E. Menuel	No. 32	142
,, ,, Lhermitte's Improved	H. Everling	Bay	2
,, ,, Rotary	Lawrence Bros. ...	,,	13
Perforating Machine	C. G. Squintani & Co.	Centre of	Gt. Hall
Perforator, Patent Rotary Round-Hole	Latham Bros. ...	No. 33	155
Perforating Presses	Baddeley & Reynolds	No. 25	42
,, ,, ...	S. Mordan & Co. ...	No. 35	189
,, ,, ...	B. Sulman	,,	188
Plates and Bars, Cutting, Improved Composition	Grey & Marten ...	No. 36	203
Plates, Brass Engine	A. Sheldon	No. 30	115
,, Engine	Crookes, Roberts & Co.	,,	117
Presses, Eyeleting	S. Mordan & Co. ...	No. 35	189

EXHIBIT.	EXHIBITOR.	Row.	No. of Space.
Presses, Hydraulic	J. Richmond & Co. ...	No. 31	124
„ Perforating	S. Mo dan & Co. ...	No. 35	18J
„ „	B. Sulman	„	188
„ „	Baddeley & Reynolds	No. 25	42
Pressing Machine, Patent Process and Improved Dry	M'Cormick & Begg ...	North Side	38
Press, Stamping	T. Kendell	Bay	1
Pulp Refiner	G. Tidcombe & Son	Bays	15 & 16
Quire Folding Machine.	Lawrence Bros. ...	Bay	13
„ „	J. Richmond & Co. ...	No. 31	124
„ „ Richmond & Co.'s	J. E. H. Andrew ...	Bay	18
Rag Engine, Model of	H. Cooke & Co. ...	No. 30	116
„ „ Sharpening Machine for	B. Donkin & Co. ...	„	118
Railway Ticket Chopping Machine ...	Waterlow & Sons, Ltd.	North Side	34
„ „ Destroying „ ...	„ „	„	„
„ „ Long Shearing „ ...	„ „	„	„
Reay's Patent Envelope Cutting Machine.	J. Richmond & Co. ...	No. 31	124
„ „ „ „ Folding Machine.	„ „ ...	„	„
Refiner, Pulp	G. Tidcombe & Son ...	Bays	15 & 16
Richmond & Co.'s Quire Folding Machine	J. E. H. Andrew ...	„	18
Roll, Calender, Finished Chilled English Iron.	Masson & Scott ...	East Side	28
Roll Carriages, Improved "Universal," Dandy.	T. J. Marshall & Co. ...	No. 29	96
Roller Bars	Crookes, Roberts &Co.	No. 30	117
Rolls, Dandy	T. J. Marshall & Co.	No. 29	96
Rotary Millboard Cutting Machine ...	W. Crosland	Bay	14
„ Perforating Machine... ...	Lawrence Bros. ...	„	13
„ Round Hole Perforator, Patent.	Latham Bros. ...	No. 33	155
„ Scoring Machine	W. Crosland	Bay	14
Round Hole Perforator, Patent Rotary.	Latham Bros. ...	No. 33	155
Scoring and Cutting Machine Combined.	W. Crosland	Bay	14
„ Machine	J. Salmon	„	4
„ „ Rotary	W. Crosland	„	14
Self Clamp Cutting Machines, "Diamond."	Hazell, Watson and Viney.	„	1

Exhibit.	Exhibitor.	Row.	No. of Space.
Self Clamping Cutting Machine, Undercut.	Lawrence Bros. ...	,,	13
Self Clamp Guillotine Cutting Machine, " Express."	Furnival & Co. ...	East Side	26
Sewing and Folding Combination Machine, Book.	Ihlee & Horne ...	Bay	11
Sharpening and Grooving Machine ...	A. Sheldon	No. 30	115
,, Machine for Rag Engine	B. Donkin & Co. ...	,,	118
Stamping Press	T. Kendell	Bay	1
Steam Cook and Knee for Drying Cylinders	J. Sturrock & Son ...	No. 30	120
S rainer...	J. Bertram & Son ...	North Side	37
Strainer Frame, Flat Jogging ...	H. Watson & Son ...	No. 30	121
,, Ibotsou's Patent	G. Tidcombe & Son...	Bays	15 & 16
,, of Knotter Plates ...	G. & W. Bertram ...	North Side	32
,, Plates, Copper and Brass...	G. Tidcombe & Son...	Bays	15 & 16
T ree-Side Cutting Machine... ...	H. Everling	Bay	2
Ticket, Railway, Chopping Machine	Waterlow & Sons,Ltd.	North Side	34
,, ,, Destroying ,,	,, ,,	,,	,,
,, ,, Long Shearing ,,	,, ,,	,,	,,
Trimming Machine	Latham Bros. ...	No. 33	155
Under-cut Self Clamping Cutting Machine.	Lawrence Bros. ...	Bay	13
" Universal " Dandy Roll Carriages, Improved.	T. J. Marshall & Co.	Row 29	96
" Universal " Job and Label Cutting Machine.	Furnival and Co. ...	East Side	26
Vertical and Diagonal Paper Cutting Machine.	W. Conisbee & Son ...	No. 33	154
"Victory" Guillotine Cutting Machine	J. Salmon	Bay	4
Water-marked Papers, Machine for Cutting.	G. Tidcombe & Son...	Bays	15 & 16
Wire Guide, Anderson's	J. Sturrock & Son ...	No. 30	120
,, ,, Brace's	,, ...	,,	,,
,, ,, Improved Patent ...	,, ...	,,	,,
Wires, Paper Machine	T. J. Marshall & Co. .	No. 29	96

III.—MOTIVE MACHINERY.

Exhibit.	Exhibitor.	Row.	No. of Space.
Belting, Leather	R. H. Williams & Sons	West Side	38 c
,, Vulcanized India Rubber ...	T. J. Marshall & Co.	No. 29	96
Bisschop's Gas Engines	J. E. H. Andrew ...	Bay	18
Boiler and Engine Combined ...	R. H. Williams & Sons	West Side	38 c
Boiler and Engine Combined, Outridge's Patent	C. G. Squintani & Co.	Centre of	Gt. Hall
Boiler and Engine, "Talbot" Combined	Proctor & Wallis ...	Bay	6
Boilers, Steam	R. H. Williams & Sons	West Side	38 c
Brown's Patent Caloric Engine ...	Greenwood & Batley	North Side	31
Caloric Engine, Brown's Patent ...	,, ,,	,, ,,	,,
Edwards' New Patent Improved Gas Engine	Proctor & Wallis ...	Bay	6
Engine	J. J. Seekings & Co....	No. 32	149
Engine and Boiler Combined ...	R. H. Williams & Sons	West Side	38 c
Engine and Boiler Combined, Outridge's Patent	C. G. Squintani & Co.	Centre of	Gt. Hall
Engine and Boiler, "Talbot" Combined	Proctor & Wallis ...	Bay	6
Engine, Bisschop's Gas	J. E. H. Andrew ...	,,	18
,, Brown's Patent Caloric ...	Greenwood & Batley	North Side	31
,, Edwards' Improved Gas ...	Proctor & Wallis ...	Bay	6
,, Fixed, with Locomotive Boiler	Robey & Co.	No. 35	193
,, Frictionless Steam	J. Turnbull, Jun. ...	Bay	24
,, Horizontal	General Engine and Boiler Co.	No. 32	151
,, ,, "Express" ...	General Engine and Boiler Co.	,,	,,
,, Horizontal Fixed	Robey & Co.	No. 35	193
,, ,. ,, ...	Marshall, Sons & Co.	West Side	39
,, ,, Steam ...	E. S. Hindley ...	No. 31	135
,, Lehmann's Hot Air ...	W. H. Bailey & Co....	No. 36	201
,, "Otto" Silent Gas... ...	Crossley Bros. ...	Bay	23
,, Oxy-Hydro Gas	H. S. Cropper & Co....	No. 36	195
,, Stationary	Marshall, Sons & Co.	West Side	39
,, Vertical	Robey & Co.	No. 35	193
,, ,, ...	Marshall, Sons & Co.	West Side	39
,, ,, ...	E. S. Hindley ...	No. 31	135

Exhibit.	Exhibitor.	Row.	No. of Space.
Engine, with Gas Heated Boiler ...	General Engine and Boiler Co.	No. 32	151
Frictionless Steam Engine	J. Turnbull, Jun. ...	Bay	24
Gas Engines, Bisschop's	J. E. H. Andrew ...	„	18
„ „ Edwards' New Patent Improved.	Proctor & Wallis ...	„	6
„ „ "Otto" Silent ...	Crossley Bros. ...	Bay	23
„ Engine, Oxy-Hydro	H. S. Cropper & Co....	No. 36	195
„ Motor, The "Leicester" ...	C. Linford & Co. ...	No. 32	150
Holloway's Apparatus for working Paper Making Machines.	G. Tidcombe & Son...	Bays	15 & 16
Horizontal "Express" Engine ...	General Engine and Boiler Co.	No. 32	151
„ Fixed „ ...	Robey & Co.	No. 35	193
„ „ Engine	Marshall, Sons & Co..	West Side	39
„ Steam Engine	E. S. Hindley ...	No. 31	135
„ „ „	General Engine and Boiler Co.	No. 32	151
Hot Air Engine, Lehmann's ...	W. H. Bailey & Co. ...	No. 36	201
Lehmann's Hot Air Engine	„	„	„
"Leicester Gas Motor," The... ...	C. Linford and Co. ...	No. 32	150
Lubricator	Engelbert and Co. ...	No. 36	196
Oilers, Machine	B. G. Brown and Co.	No. 29	98
"Otto" Silent Gas Engine	Crossley Bros. ...	Bay	23
Outridge's Patent Engine and Boiler Combined	C. G. Squintani & Co.	Centre of	Gt. Hall
Oxy-Hydro Gas Engine	H. S. Cropper & Co.	No. 36	195
Paper Making Machines Holloway's Apparatus for Working.	G. Tidcombe and Son	Bays	15 & 16
Safety Valve	J. Sturrock & Son ...	No. 30	120
Stationary Steam Engine	Marshall, Sons & Co.	West Side	39
"Talbot" Combined Steam Engine and Boiler.	Proctor & Wallis ...	Bay	6
Valve, Safety	J. Sturrock & Son ...	No. 30	120
Vertical Steam Engine	Marshall, Sons & Co.	West Side	39
„ „ „	E. S. Hindley ...	No. 31	135
„ „ „	Robey & Co.	No. 35	193

IV.—TYPE, COMPOSITOR'S ROOM FURNITURE, &c.

EXHIBIT.	EXHIBITOR.	Row.	No. of Space.
Adjustable Steel Gauge Pins and Feed Guides, Megill's.	J. L. Chapin & Co. ...	Centre of	Gt. Hall
American Fancy Type	,, ...	,,	,,
Brass Rules	W. Notting	Bay	7
Brushes...	J. Masters	No. 29	103
Cabinet, "Eagle" Printer's	J. L. Chapin & Co. ...	Centre of	Gt. Hall
Case Rack, Folding	F. Ullmer	Bay	21
Case Racks	Day & Collins ...	,,	8
Cases	,, ...	,,	,,
,, ...	F. Ullmer	,,	21
,, Type	J. C. Paul	No. 29	105
,, ,, ...	Marr Type Founding Co., Limited ...	No. 30	112
Chases	E. Menuel	No. 32	142
,, Wrought Iron	F. Ullmer	Bay	21
Circles and Ovals	C. F. Moore	No. 31	131
Composing Frames	Day & Collins ...	Bay	8
,, Sticks	,, ...	,,	,,
,, ,, ...	C. F. Moore	No. 31	131
,, ,, ...	E. Menuel	No. 32	142
Dashes	C. F. Moore	No. 31	131
Designs, Ornamental, in Brass ...	W. Notting	Bay	7
"Eagle," Printer's Cabinet	J. L. Chapin & Co. ...	Centre of	Gt. Hall
Fancy Type, American	,, ,, ...	,,	,,
Feed Guides and Gauge Pins, "Megill's" Adjustable Steel	,, ,, ...	,,	,,
Folding Case Rack	F. Ullmer	Bay	21
Forme Racks	Day & Collins ...	,,	8
Frame, Imposing Surface and ...	F. Ullmer	,,	21
Frames	Marr Type Founding Co.	No. 30	112
Frame with Rack and 9 half cases ...	F. Ullmer	Bay	21
Frames, Composing	Day & Collins ...	,,	8
Galley Letter Board Racks	,, ...	,,	8

Exhibit.	Exhibitor.	Row.	No. of Space.
Galley Proof Presses, Improved Lever and Roller	W. Notting	Bay	7
Galleys	F. Ullmer	,,	21
,, ...	C. F. Moore	No. 31	131
,, ...	E. Menuel	No. 32	142
Gauge Pins	C. G. Squintani & Co.	Centre of	Gt. Hall
,, ,, & Feed Guides, "Megill's," Adjustable Steel	J. L. Chapin & Co. ...	,,	,,
Imposing Surfaces	Day & Collins ...	Bay	8
,, ,, and Frame	F. Ullmer	,,	21
Improved Lever and Roller Galley Proof Press	W. Notting	,,	7
Joinery, Printers'	J. C. Paul	No. 29	105
Lead and Rule Cutter, "Little Giant"	J. L. Chapin and Co.	Centre of	Gt. Hall
,, ,, ,,	C. G. Squintani & Co.	,,	,,
Letter and Galley Board Racks ...	Day and Collins ...	Bay	8
"Little Giant" Rule and Lead Cutter	J. L. Chapin and Co.	Centre of	Gt. Hall
,, ,, ,,	C. G. Squintani & Co.	,,	,,
Locking-up Apparatus	E. Menuel	No. 32	142
,, ,,	W. H. Caslon & Co. ...	No. 36	205
,, ,, "Twin Quoins"	C. G. Squintani & Co.	Centre of	Gt. Hall
Mallets	Day and Collins ...	Bay	8
Megill's Adjustable Steel Guage Pins and Feed Guides.	J. L. Chapin & Co. ...	Centre of	Gt. Hall
Ornamental Designs in Brass ...	W. Notting	Bay	7
Ovals and Circles	C. F. Moore	No. 31	131
Planers	Day & Collins ...	Bay	8
Plates, Zinc	Guttenberg Wood Type Co., Limited.	No. 29	104
Proof Presses, Improved Lever and Roller Galley.	W Notting	Bay	7
Rack, Case Folding	F. Ullmer	,,	21
Racks, Case	Day & Collins ...	,,	8
,, Forme	,, ,, ...	,,	,,
,, Galley and Letter Board ...	,, ,, ...	,,	,,
Reglet and Furniture	,, ,, ...	,,	,,
Rule and Lead Cutter, "Little Giant"	J. L. Chapin & Co. ...	Centre of	Gt. Hall
,, ,, ,, ,, ,,	C. G. Scuintani & Co.	,,	,,
Rules	Marr Type Founding Co., Limited.	No. 30	112

EXHIBIT.	EXHIBITOR.	Row.	No. of Space.
Rules	C. F. Moore	No. 31	131
Rules, Brass	W. Notting	Bay	7
Shooting Sticks	E. Menuel	No. 32	142
Sticks, Composing	C. F. Moore	No. 31	131
,, ,, ...	Day & Collins ...	Bay	8
,, Shooting and Composing ...	E. Menuel	No. 32	142
Type, American Fancy	J. L. Chapin & Co. ...	Centre of Gt.	Hall
,, Cases	J. C. Paul	No. 29	105
,, Cast Brass	E. Menuel	No. 32	142
,, ,, ...	M. Marx	No. 33	163
,, Casting Machine	C. Morton	No. 29	106
,, in Founts	,, ...	,,	,,
,, ,, ...	Marr Type Founding Co,, Limited	No. 30	112
,, ,, ...	W. H. Caslon & Co....	No. 36	205
,, Solid Rubber	City Rubber Stamp Co.	No. 34	176
,, Wood	Guttenburg Wood Type Co., Limited	No. 29	104
,, ,, ...	J. L. Chapin & Co. ...	Centre of Gt.	Hall
,, Wood, Page's	Durable Prirter Roller Co.	No. 30	114
" Twin Quoins " Locking-up Apparatus	C. G. Squintani & Co.	Centre of Gt.	Hall
Wetting Troughs	Day & Collins ...	Bay	8
Wood Letter Bulks	,, ...	,,	,,
,, Type	J. L. Chapin & Co....	Centre of	Gt. Hall
,, ,, ...	Guttenberg Wood Type Co., Lim.	No. 29	104
, ,, Page's	Durable Printer Roller Co.	No. 30	114
Zihc Plates	Guttenberg Wood Tyᵢe Co.	No. 29	104

V.—MATERIALS, RAW AND FINISHED.

EXHIBIT.	EXHIBITOR.	Row.	No. of Space.
" Acmé " Composition	Fairholme & Co. ...	Bay	23
Alkali, Refined	W. G. Taylor & Co....	No. 35	181
Alloys of Antimony	Grey & Marten ...	No. 36	203
Alum	W. G. Taylor & Co....	No. 35	181
„	A. Zumbeck & Co. ...	No. 36	200
Aluminous Cake	„ ...	„	„
Ambré, Papier	H. Everling	Bay	2
Aniline Colours	A. Zumbeck & Co. ...	No. 36	200
„ Cycloids	W. C. Hood	No. 26	67
„ Dyes	„	„	„
Antimonial Lead	Grey & Marten ..	No. 36	203
Ash, Soda	W. G. Taylor & Co....	No. 35	181
Aspen and Bleached Pine Pulps ...	Grellingen Wood Pulp Company.	No. 25	45
Aspen Paste	A. Zumbeck & Co. ...	No. 36	200
Asphalte Paper Roofing	Lehmann & Sankey...	No. 34	173
Baggings, Jute...	A. Wertheim & Co. ...	No. 25	49
Beltonford Paper	A. Annandale ...	East Side	29
Black Lead, or Graphite	E. Wolff & Son ...	Bay	9
Blacks, Vegetable and Spirit... ...	Battley & Co.... ...	No. 36	202
Bleached Pine Pulps	Grellingen Wood Pulp Company.	No. 25	45
Bleaching Powder	W. G. Taylor & Co....	No. 35	181
Blottings, Coloured	T. B. Ford	No. 34	171
„ 428 Mill, White	„	„	„
Boards, Wood Pulp	I. Spiro & Son ...	No. 25	51
„ „ „	F. Schroeder & Co. ...	No. 35	192
Bronze Powders	Zorn, Bahnson & Co...	No. 36	197
„ „	Stotz & Winter ...	No. 29	102
„ „	Weinschenk & Co. ...	„	99
„ „	Coates Bros.	„	97
„ „	W. Ehrman	No. 28	93
Browns (Paper)	C. Davidson & Sons...	No. 26	66
Carbonic Papers	Field & Tuer	No. 26	71
Caustic Soda	W. G. Taylor & Co....	No. 35	181

Exhibit.	Exhibitor.	Row.	No. of Space.
China Clay	Roche Goonbarrow China Clay Co., Ltd.	No. 27	78
,, ...	W. G. Taylor & Co....	No. 35	181
Clay, China	,, ...	,,	,,
,, ...	Roche Goonbarrow China Clay Co., Ltd.	No. 27	,,
Coloured Paper...	Henggeler & Co. ...	No. 25	47
Colours	Stotz & Winter ...	No. 29	102
,, ...	Zorn, Bahnson & Co.	No. 36	197
"Compo-Lithograph"	Compo-Litho. Co. ...	No. 28	91
Composition, "Acmé"	Fairholme & Co. ...	Bay	23
,, "Speciale" Roller ...	Sir C. Reed & Sons ...	West Side	38B
Compo, The "Durable"	Durable Printer Roller Co., Limited	No. 30	114
Crystal Soda	W. G. Taylor & Co. ...	No. 35	181
Cycloids, Aniline	W. C. Hood	No. 26	67
Dyes, Aniline	,, ...	,,	,,
,, Household	F. Mordan & Co. ...	No. 28	87
,, Liquid	E. J. Hollidge ...	No. 26	59
Esparto	W. G. Taylor & Co. ...	No. 35	181
Farina	,, ...	,,	,,
Felt	J. C. Humphreys ...	South Side	40A
,, Paper	C. Davidson & Sons, Limited	No. 26	66
Feltine	Ihlee & Horne ...	Bay	11
Galvanized Iron Roofing	J. C. Humphreys ...	South Side	40A
Gelatine...	W. C. Hood	No. 26	67
,, ...	J. B. Cumming ...	No. 32	145
,, ...	Clark, Thackray & Co.	No. 33	158
German Linen and Cotton Rags ...	J. Jacobson & Co. ...	No. 25	44
Glazed Papers	C. Davidson & Sons, Limited.	No. 26	66
Glue	W. C. Hood	,,	67
,, ...	J. B. Cumming ...	No. 32	145
,, ...	Clark, Thackray & Co.	No. 33	158
,, Household	F. Mordan & Co. ...	No. 28	87
Gold Foil	H. Erhardt	No. 35	187
Graphite, or Black Lead	E. Wolff & Son ...	Bay	9
Greys	C. Davidson & Sons, Limited.	No. 26	66

EXHIBIT.	EXHIBITOR.	Row.	No. of space.
Gum, Double Strength	F. Mordan & Co. ...	No. 28	87
,, Office	,, ,,	,,	,,
Hide Cuttings	J. B. Cumming ...	No. 32	145
Indigo Dyed Rags, Scoured	F. V. Kallab	No. 25	52
,, Rags freed from..	,, ...	,,	,,
,, Regained from Indigo Dyed Rags	,, ...	,,	,,
,, ,, ,, Rags, Tissues dyed with.	,, ...	,,	,,
Ink, American Printing	Durable Printer Roller Company.	No. 30	114
,, Black and Coloured	C. Schramm	No. 27	76A
,, Coloured	F. Mordan & Co. ...	No. 28	87
,, Copying	,, ,, ...	,,	,,
,, "City of London" Marking ...	,, ,, ...	,,	,,
,, Dichroic Writing, &c.	W. H. Hayden & Co.	No. 33	161
,, Endorsing, for India-rubber Stamps.	F. Mordan & Co. ...	No. 28	87
,, Letter-press	Coates Bros.	No. 29	97
,, Liquid Printing	W. C. Hood	No. 26	67
,, Lithographic	Coates Bros.	No. 29	97
,, ,, and Letter-press ...	Zorn, Bahnson & Co.	No. 36	197
,, Marking	E. Wolff & Son ...	No. 31	129
,, ,, ...	M. A. Bond	,,	134
,, Multiple	F. Mordan & Co. ...	No. 28	87
,, Perfumed Marking	,, ,, ...	,,	,,
,, Powders	E. J. Hollidge ...	No. 26	59
,, ,, Soluble	F. Mordan & Co. ...	No. 28	87
,, ,, ,, Coloured ...	,, ,, ...	,,	,,
,, Ruling	,, ,, ...	,,	,,
,, Sensitive	Durable Printers' Roller Company.	No. 30	114
Inks for Rubber Stamps	City Rubber Stamp Co.	No. 34	176
Inks, Writing and Copying	G. Toiray	No. 36	198
Ink, Ticket	F. Mordan & Co. ...	No. 28	87
,, Writing	,, ,, ..	,,	,,
Iron Roofing, Galvanized	J. C. Humphreys ...	South Side	40A
Japanese Paper	Field & Tuer	No. 26	71
Jute	W. G. Taylor & Co....	No. 35	181
,, Baggings	A. Wertheim & Co. ...	No. 25	49

Exhibit.	Exhibitor.	Row.	No. of Space.
Lead, Antimonial	Grey & Marten ...	No. 36	203
„ Black, or Graphite	E. Wolff & Son ...	Bay	9
„ for Type Founders	Grey & Marten ..	No. 36	203
„ Nitrate and Sugar of	A. Zumbeck & Co. ...	„	200
Leaf Metals	Weinschenk & Co. ...	No. 29	99
„	Stotz & Winter ...	„	102
Leatherette	Ihlee & Horne ...	Bay	11
Manifold Papers	Field & Tuer... ...	No. 26	71
Manillas	C. Davidson & Son, Ltd.	„	66
Manilla Tissues	Field & Tuer	„	71
Material for founding Roller Moulds	W. Conisbee & Son...	No. 33	154
Metals, Leaf	Weinschenk & Co. ...	No. 29	99
„	Stotz & Winter ...	„	102
Middles	Lehmann & Sankey...	No. 34	173
„	J. Rowney	No. 32	140
„	C. Davidson & Son, Ltd.	No. 26	66
„ Wood	C. F. Waern & Co. ...	No. 25	43
Millboards	J. Rowney	No. 32	140
„	Lehmann & Sankey...	No. 34	173
Molina Cerulea	N. G. Richardson ...	No. 35	182
News	J. Dickinson & Co. ...	No. 27	72
„	E. Lloyd	No. 35	183
Nitrate of Lead...	A. Zumbeck & Co. ...	No. 36	200
Nut Galls	F. Mordan & Co. ...	No. 28	87
Packing Paper	I. Spiro & Son ...	No. 25	51
„ „ Waterproof	„ ...	„	„
Paper Beltonford	A. Annandale ...	East Side	29
„ Brown	C. Davidson & Sons...	No. 26	26
„ Carbonic	Field & Tuer... ...	No. 26	71
„ Coloured	Henggeler & Co. ...	No. 25	47
„ Glazed	C. Davidson & Son, Limited	No. 26	66
„ Japanese	Field & Tuer... ...	„	71
„ Japanese and Chinese ...	Londos & Co. ...	No. 33	153
„ Makers' Materials	Gebrüder Lewy ...	No. 27	75
„ Manifold	Field & Tuer... ...	No. 26	71
, News	E. Lloyd	No. 35	183
„ Packing...	I. Spiro & Son ...	No. 25	51

Exhibit.	Exhibitor.	Row.	No. of Space.
Paper Packing...	Lehmann & Sankey...	No. 34	173
,, Plate and Lithographic ...	Mendip Paper Mills Co.	No. 26	63
,, Printing	F. Schroeder & Co. ...	No. 35	192
,, ,, ...	I. Spiro & Son ...	No. 25	51
,, ,, and Writing, &c. ...	Cameron & Ferguson	No. 31	133
,, Straw	C. Siou & Co. ...	No. 25	46
,, Turkey Mill	Hollingworth & Co....	Bay	15 & 16
,, Vat	G. F. Busbridge & Co.	,,	53
,, Waterproof Packing	I. Spiro & Son ...	,,	51
,, White	C. Davidson & Son, Limited	No. 26	66
,, Wood Pulp	I. Spiro & Son· ...	No. 25	51
,, Wrapping	C. Davidson & Son, Limited	No. 26	66
,, Writings, Printings, &c. ...	J. Rowney	No. 32	140
Papier Ambré	H. Everling... ...	Bay	2
Parchment, Vegetable	H. Erhardt & Co. ...	No. 35	187
Paste, Aspen	A. Zumbeck & Co. ...	No. 36	200
,, Pine	,, ,,	,,	,,
Pine, Paste	,, ,,	,,	,,
,, Pulp, Aspen and Bleached ...	Grellingen Wood Pulp Co.	No. 25	45
Pliable Wood for Covering Books ...	Ihlee & Horne ...	Bay	11
Powder, Bleaching	W. G. Taylor & Co....	No. 35	181
Powders, Bronze	Zorn, Bahnson & Co.	No. 36	197
,, ,, ...	W. Ehrmann ...	No. 28	93
,, ,, ...	Coates Bros.	No. 29	97
,, ,, ...	Weinschenk & Co. ...	,,	99
,, ,, ...	Stotz & Winter ...	,,	102
,, Ink	E. J. Hollidge ...	No. 26	59
Printings	J. Dickinson & Co. ...	No. 27	72
,, ...	Mendip Paper Mills Co.	No. 26	63
Printings	I. Spiro & Son ...	No. 25	51
Pulp, Aspen and Bleached Pine ...	Grellingen Wood Pulp Co.	,,	45
,, Straw	Heyer & Pistor ...	No. 29	108
,, ,, ...	G. F. Green & Co. ...	No. 30	119
,, Wood	A. Zumbeck & Co. ...	No. 36	200

Exhibit	Exhibitor.	Row.	No. of Space.
Pulp, Wood	W. G. Taylor & Co. ...	No. 35	181
,, ,, ...	G . F. Green & Co. ...	No. 30	119
,, ,, ...	C. F. Waerne & Co....	No. 25	43
,, ,, Chemically Prepared ...	,, ,, ...	,,	,,
,, ,, ,, ,, ...	W. Hamer	No. 34	172
,, ,, Mechanically ,, ...	,, ...	,,	,,
" Purple Melic Grass "	N. G. Richardson ...	No. 35	182
Rags	Gebrüder Lewy ...	No. 27	75
,, Foreign	W. G. Taylor & Co. ...	No. 35	181
,, Freed from Indigo	F. V. Kallab	No. 25	52
,, German Linen and Cotton ...	J. Jacobson & Co. ...	,,	44
,, Indigo regained from Indigo dyed	F. V. Kallab	,,	52
,, Linen and Cotton	A. Wertheim & Co. ...	,,	49
,, Scoured Indigo Dyed	F. V. Kallab	,,	52
Roller Moulds, Material for Founding	W. Conisbee & Son ...	No. 33	154
,, Composition " Specialé " ...	Lehmann & Sankey...	No. 34	173
Roofing, Asphalte Paper	Sir C. Reed & Sons...	West Side	38B
,, Galvanized Iron	J. C. Humpheys ...	South Side	40A
Rosin	W. G. Taylor & Co. ...	No. 35	181
Sealing Wax (*Vide* Wax)	F. Mordan & Co. ...	No. 28	87
Shellac	,, ,, ...	,,	,,
Soda Ash	W. G. Taylor & Co....	No. 35	181
Soda Caustic	,, ,, ...	,,	,,
,, Crystal	,, ,, ...	,,	,,
" Specialé " Roller Composition ...	,, ,, ...	,,	,,
Starch	Sir C. Reed & Sons...	West Side	38B
Strawboard	F. Schroeder & Co. ...	,,	192
,, ...	Lehmann & Sankey...	No. 34	173
Straw Paper	C. Siou & Co. ...	No. 25	46
,, Pulp	Heyer & Pistor ...	No. 29	108
Sugar of Lead	A. Zumbeck	No. 36	200
Tin	Grey & Marten ...	No. 36	203
Tinfoil	H. Erhardt	No. 35	187
Tissues, Dyed with Indigo regained from Rags.	F. V. Kallab	No. 25	52
Tissues, Manilla	Field & Tuer... ...	No. 26	71
Ultramarine	W. C. Wood	,,	67
,, ...	G. Botelberge & Co....	No. 27	77
,, ...	Stotz & Winter ...	No. 29	102

Exhibit.	Exhibitor.	Row.	No. of Space.
Varnishes	Coates Bros.	No. 29	97
Vat Paper	G. F. Busbridge & Co.	No. 25	53
Vegetable Parchment	H. Erhardt	No. 35	187
Vermilion	W. H. Atkinson ...	No. 25	56
,, ...	F. Mordan & Co. ...	No. 28	87
Waterproof Packing Paper	I. Spiro & Son ..	No. 25	51
Wax, Bank of England	F. Mordan & Co. ...	No. 28	87
,, Bottling	,, ...	,,	,,
,, Druggists'	,, ...	,,	,,
,, Engravers'	,, ...	,,	,,
,, Hard India	,, ...	,,	,,
,, Parcel	,, ...	,,	,,
,, Pipe Makers'	,, ...	,,	,,
,, Post Office	,, ...	,,	,,
,, Sealing	,, ...	,,	,
,, used for Great Seal of England	,, ...	,,	,,
Wood for Binding Purposes, Sala's ...	Ihlee & Horne ...	Bay	10
,, Middles	C. F. Waerne & Co. ...	No. 25	43
,, Pliable for Covering Books ...	Ihlee & Horne ...	Bay	10
,, Pulp	C. F. Waerne & Co. ...	No. 25	43
,, ,, ...	G. F. Green & Co. ...	No. 30	119
,, ,, ...	W. G. Taylor & Co. ...	No. 35	181
,, ,, ...	A. Zumbeck & Co. ...	No. 36	200
,, ,, Bleached Chemical ...	G. F. Green & Co. ...	No. 30	119
,, ,, Boards	Schroeder & Co. ...	No. 35	192
,, ,, ,, ...	I. Seiro & Son ...	No. 25	51
,, ,, Chemically Prepared ...	C. F. Waerne & Co. ...	,,	43
,, ,, ,, ,, ...	W. Hamer	No. 34	172
,, ,, Mechanically ,, ...	,, ...	,,	,,
,, ,, Paper	I. Spiro & Son ...	No. 25	51
,, ,, Unbleached Chemical ...	G. F. Green & Co. ...	No. 30	119
Wrapping Paper	Davidson & Son, Ltd.	No. 26	63

VI.—MISCELLANEA.

BOOKBINDING APPLIANCES— BOOKBINDING MACHINERY — BOOKS — ENGRAVINGS — MISCELLANEOUS MACHINERY — PERIODICALS—PROCESSES— SCIENTIFIC INSTRUMENTS—STATIONERY, &c.

N.B.—In consequence of the pressure on our space the cross references have been suppressed in this portion of the Guide, although every means has been taken to render consultation easy. The large number of minor Exhibits has also prevented the indexing of EACH SINGLE ITEM, and they have consequently been grouped under the various " SUNDRIES " and their particular generic headings.

EXHIBIT.	EXHIBITOR.	Row.	No. of Space.
Advertising Signs	H. Bevis	South Side	40
Air-diffusing Fire Bar, Model of ...	H. Cooke & Co. ...	No. 30	116
Almanacs, Pictorial	A. Cook	No. 25	57
American Specialities	Lawrence Bros. ...	No. 30	113
Argands, Low-Pressure	G. E. Webster & Co...	Bay	6
Bags, Paper	C. Davidson & Sons, Limited	No. 26	66
Band and Circular Saw Bench ...	E. S. Hindley ...	No. 31	135
Bands, Elastic...	Perry & Co., Ltd. ...	Centre of	Gt. Hall
Banners...	H. Bevis	South Side	40
Binding, Cloth...	R. Peck	Bay	19
„ Specimens of	Eyre & Spottiswoode	No. 27	84
„ Specimens of Vellum ...	Smith & Wolff ...	No. 31	128
Bookbinders' Press	W. Vickery	No. 32	147
Bookbinding Machinery (various) ...	J. Richmond & Co. ...	No. 31	124
„ Specimens of	E. Watson	No. 26	69
Book, Printed	Roche Goonbarrow, China Clay Co.,Ltd.	No. 27	78
„ „	J. L. Chapin & Co. ...	Centre of	Gt. Hall
„ Support, Mason's Adjustable	„ ...	„	„
Books, Account	Cameron & Ferguson	No. 31	133
„ „	W. Hawtin & Son ...	No. 33	162
„ „	H. Mead	„	54

Exhibit.	Exhibitor.	Row.	No. of Space.
Books, Account, &c.	W. Collins, Sons & Co., Limited	No. 25	41
„ Printed	J. Dickenson & Co....	No. 27	72
„ Specimen	J. L. Chapin & Co. ...	Centre of	Gt. Hall
Borders, Floral and Illuminated ...	Riddle & Couchman...	Bay	20
„ in Fancy Papers	R. Dettelbach ...	No. 29	110
Bronze, Fancy Articles in	J. E. Webster & Co....	Bay	6
Bronzing Machine	J. Salmon	„	4
Cabinet Ware, Stationers'	Perry & Co., Limited	Centre of	Gt. Hall
Cards, Playing, &c.	J. English & Co. ...	No. 26	61
„ „	C. Goodall & Son ...	No. 33	152
„ for Jacquard Looms	Avalon Leather Board Co.	No. 26	62
„ Memory	J. Smith & Co. ...	„	68
„ Show, &c.	Armitage & Ibbetson	No. 34	170
„ Hand Painted	C. W. Stidstone ...	„	175
„ Floral and Hand Painted ...	W. Luks	No. 35	90
Caxton Relics and Memorials ...	J. S. Hodson... ...	No. 26	70
Chromo-Lithographs	Gow, Butterfield & Co.	„	60
„ „	T. Taylor	„	70
„ „	J. Nicholson	No. 33	157
„ „	Riddle & Couchman	Bay	20
„ Lithography	Eyre & Spottiswoode	No. 27	84
„ „ Specimens of...	C. Goodall & Son ...	No. 33	152
„ „ „ ...	Th. Dupuy & Sons...	No. 35	184
„ Portraits	R. Tuck	No. 27	82
Clocks, American	Perry & Co., Limited	Centre of	Gt Hall
Cloth, Bookbinders'	Law, Sons & Co. ...	No. 33	159
„ Gold and Silver	„ ...	„	„
Colour Boxes	W. Collins Son, & Co., Ltd.	No. 25	41
„ Printing, Specimens of ...	T. Hildesheimer & Co.	No. 31	132
Curiosities, Typographical	Field & Tuer... ...	No. 26	71
Curling Papers...	A. Fieget	No. 27	74
Cutlery, Pocket	Perry & Co., Limited	Centre of	Gt. Hall
Dasymeter, Horack	H. Everling	Bay	2
Deckle Straps, Red Rubber	T. J. Marshall & Co.	No. 29	96
Desks	W. Collins, Son, & Co., Limited.	No. 25	41
„ School	R. Troughton ...	No. 32	148

Exhibit.	Exhibitor.	Row.	No. of Space.
Diaries	Campbell, D. & Son...	No. 33	160
Drawings and Photographs	Printers' Pension, etc., Corporation ...	No. 26	70
Fancy Articles...	S. Mordan & Co. ...	No. 35	189
,, Goods	D. S. Stacy	Centre of	Gt. Hall
Feed Water Heater	General Engine and Boiler Company.	No. 32	151
Files (Letter and Invoice, &c.) ...	Cameron, Amberg and Company.	No. 36	194
Fine Art Publications...	W. Luks	No. 35	90
Flower Boxes	H. Rees & Co., Ltd.	No. 27	81
Frames	Walmesley & Lewis ...	Bay.	* * *
Freeman's Journal	E. Dwyer-Gray, M.P.	No. 29	101
Furniture, Counting House	J. Guy & Sons ...	No. 33	164
Gas Lighting, "Duplex" System of	G. E. Webster & Co....	Bay	6
Gauges, Pressure	,, ...	,,	,,
Globes	,, ...	,,	,,
Governors	,, ...	,,	,,
Graining Boards	W. Vickery	No. 32	147
House, Portable Iron, for Printers ...	J. C. Humphreys ...	South Side	40a
Inkstands	L. Hardtmuth & Co...	No. 27	79
Illuminating	Baddeley & Reynolds	No. 25	42
Illuminating, Specimens of	Theyer & Hardtmuth	No. 36	206
Ink, Experiments showing the superiority of Neutral Non-corrosive over ordinary Blue-Black	F. Mordan & Co. ...	No. 28	87
Indigo, Recovering	F. V. Kallab	,,	52
,, Regaining	,, ...	,,	,,
Labels, Cloth	N. Defries & Co. ...	No. 34	179
Lead Pencils, Manufacture of ...	E. Wolff & Son ...	Bay	9
Leather Goods	W. Collins, Sons & Co., Limited.	No. 25	41
,, ...	Eyre & Spottiswoode	No. 27	84
Litho Printing on Iron	H. J. Turner... ...	No. 33	163a
Liquors, Caustic Machine for measuring	Masson & Scott ...	East Side	28
Lubricators, Needle	B. G. Brown & Co. ...	No. 29	98
Mantle Pieces	H. Rees & Co. ...	No. 27	81
Mason's Adjustable Book Support ...	J. L. Chapin & Co. ...	Centre of	Gt. Hall

Exhibit.	Exhibitor.	Row.	No. of Space.
Mathematical Instruments	W. Collins, Sons & Co., Limited.	No. 25	41
,, ,, ...	Eyre & Spottiswoode	No. 27	84
Metal Tablets, Tiles and Sheets ...	H. Rees & Co. ...	,,	81
Millboard Scale	F. Leunig & Co. ...	No. 26	65
Newspaper	Oetzman & Co. ...	No. 26	70
Newspapers, Provincial	W. H. Everett ...	No. 28	88
,, ,, ...	Proprietors	No. 29	100
Nipping Press, Bookbinders'	Fieldhouse & Elliot...	East Side	36
Oleographs	R. Tuck	No. 27	82
Ornaments in Fancy Papers	R. Dettelbach ...	No. 29	110
Paper Binders	Perry & Co., Limited	Centre of	Gt. Hall
Paper, Fancy	O. Konig & Co. ...	No. 35	186
,, Gelatine Fancy	W. Kneppers... ...	No. 27	74
,, Gold and Silver	R. Dettelbach ...	No 29	110
,, Imitation Hand-made ...	W. Monckton & Co....	No. 26	64
,, Ornamental Designs in ...	Dean & Co.	No. 31	127
,, Scale	F. Leunig & Co. ...	No. 26	65
,, ,, Pocket	,,	,,	65
,, Satin and Muslin ...	W. Kneppers... ...	No. 27	74
,, Stout Buff Coyping	Whitehead, Morris & Lowe.	No. 32	141
,, Telegraphic	Waterlow & Sons, Ltd.	East Side	34
,, Tracing and Drawing ...	Benrath & Franck ...	No. 27	76
,, Vat Drawing	G. F. Busbridge & Co.	No. 25	53
Papeteries	W. Collins, Son & Co.	,,	41
Pencil Cases	Perry & Co., Limited	Centre of	Gt. Hall
,, ,, in Gold and Silver, etc.	S. Mordan & Co. ...	No. 35	189
Pencil-making, Processes connected with	B. S. Cohen	No. 33	156
Pencils	Perry & Co., Limited	Centre of	Gt. Hall
,, Lead, manufacture of ...	E. Wolff & Son ...	Bay	9
,, ...	A. W. Faber	No. 35	185
,, etc.	E. Woolf & Son ...	No. 31	129
,, Graphite Comprimé	L. & C. Hardtmuth...	No. 27	79
,, ...	E. Wolff & Son ...	No. 31	129
Pens, Steel	Perry & Co., Limited	Centre of	Gt. Hall
,, Stylographic	Waterlow & Sons, Ltd.	East Side	34

Exhibit.	Exhibitor.	Row.	No. of Space.
Pens, Gold	F. Mordan & Co. ...	No. 28	87
„ Quill	„	„	„
Penholders	Perry & Co., Limited	Centre of	Gt. Hall
Penwipers	L. & C. Hardtmuth ...	No. 27	79
Periodicals	E. Dwyer Grey, M.P.	Bay	* * *
„	Field & Tuer	No. 26	71
„	W. Dorrington ...	No. 29	95
„	W. J. Stophill ...	„	111
„	Wyman & Sons ...	No. 36	199
Photographs	D. S. Stacy	Centre of	Gt. Hall
„	F. Frith & Co. ...	No. 26	70
„	Walmesley & Lewis ...	No. 29	101
Photo-Lithography	S. Straker & Sons ...	No. 32	89
Photo-Lithography, Specimens of ...	Unwin Bros.	No. 29	107
Photometer	G. E. Webster & Co.	Bay	6
Picture Frames	R. Tuck	No. 27	82
Portfolios	Bradbury, Wilkinson and Co.	No. 36	207
Postal Letter Scale	F. Leunig & Co. ...	No. 26	65
Printing, Specimens of	Field & Tuer	No. 26	70
Provincial Newspapers	Proprietors	No. 29	100
Printing on Iron, Litho	H. J. Turner	No. 33	163 A
Printing Machine, Drawings of ...	B. Donkin & Co. ...	No. 30	118
Printers' Specialities	Crown Steam Printing Co.	No. 31	125
		„	
Pulleys, Wrought Iron "Gap" ...	Proctor & Wallace ...	Bay	6
Purses	F. Mordan & Co. ...	No. 28	87
Publications, Time Saving	Letts, Son & Co. ...	No. 30	122
Railway Ticket Counting and Tying-up Machine	Waterlow & Sons, Ltd.	East Side	34
Railway Ticket Issue Cases and Nippers	„	„	„
Recovering, Indigo	F. V. Kallab	No. 25	52
Regaining „	„	„	„
Relief Stamping	Baddeley & Reynolds	„	42
Rounding Backs of Books, Machine for.	A. Brehmer	Bay	19
Sachets	Goode Bros.	No. 27	73

Exhibit.	Exhibitor.	Row.	No. of Space.
School Music	L. & C. Hardtmuth ...	,,	79
Scientific Instruments	J. Davis & Co. ...	No. 28	90
Sewing and Stitching Machine, Wire	A. Brehmer	Bay	19
,, Wire	R. Peck	,,	,,
Sheets, Transfer	A. E. Walker... ...	No. 32	146
Show Bills	Riddle & Couchman...	Bay	20
Slates	T. Doubble	No. 31	126
,, American	A. E. Walker... ...	No. 32	146
,, Book	L. & C. Hardtmuth ...	No. 27	79
,, Patent	D. Hammond ...	No. 34	177
Small Hands and Small Caps ...	A. Fieget	No. 27	74
Soda Ash, Machine for Crushing ..	J. Bertram & Son ...	East Side	37
Specialities on Silk and Ivory ...	C. W. Stidstone ...	No. 34	175
Stabbing Machine	W. Vickery	No. 32	147
,, ,, ...	Latham Bros. ...	No. 33	155
,, ,, Treadle	F. Ullmer	Bay	21
Stationery	D. S. Stacy	Centre of	Gt. Hal
,, ...	W. Collins, Sons & Co.	No. 25	41
,, ...	H. Mead	,,	54
,, ...	J. Smith & Co. ...	No. 26	68
,, ...	J. Dickinson & Co. ...	No. 27	72
,, ...	Speller & Preston ...	No. 34	166
,, ...	King, Son & Whittaker	,,	169
,, Machines	W. T. Lotz & Co. ...	,,	174
,, Mourning	Terry Stoneman & Co.	No. 26	70
Statuettes	D. S. Stacy	Centre of	Gt. Hall
Steel Plate Menu Cards	J. L. Chapin & Co. ...	,,	,,
,, ,, Programme Cards ...	J. L. Chapin & Co. ...	,,	,,
Stone-grinding Machine	J. Salmon	Bay	20
,, and Polishing Machine, Litho	W. Crossland ...	,,	14
Studios in Iron, for Photographers ...	J. C. Humphreys ...	South Side	40A
Sundries, Printers'	W. Notting	Bay	7
,, ,, ...	F. Ullmer	,,	21
Tablets, Enamelled Zinc	Unwin Bros.	No. 29	107
, Glass	,, ...	,	
,, Iron	,, ...	,	
,, Show	H. J. Turner... ...	No. 33	163A
,, Specialité Iron	Unwin Bros.	No. 29	107

Exhibit.	Exhibitor.	Row.	No. of Space.
Toothpicks and Pencil Cases, Pocket	W. S. Hicks	No. 35	191
Toys	Perry & Co., Limited	Centre of	Gt. Hall
Twines	T. Ironmonger & Co.	No. 28	92
Type Casting	C. Morton	No. 29	106
Valentines	Goode Bros.	No. 27	73
Waterproofed Leather Board ...	Avalon Leather Board Company.	No. 26	62
Wafers	F. Mordan & Co. ...	No. 28	84
Zinco-Typography	A. S. Cattell & Co. ...	Bay	5
Zinc Tablets, Enamelled	Unwin Bros.	No. 29	107

PREFACE.

I is, probably, not necessary to say much by way of introduction to this Catalogue, for, no doubt, in the immortal words of the stereotyped preface, the work "Speaks for itself." Still, this old practice of literary introduction—this formal survival from an age when people read little, and authors harmlessly wrote much—is very useful, for it enables certain personal matters to be recorded which, whether they are read or not, it is eminently desirable should not be neglected.

In the organization of the present Exhibition the one desire which has animated Mr. DALE has been the realization for the Printing Community of that Trade Exhibition programme, which, in some of the following pages, I have ventured to dilate upon. That this programme is one which recommends itself to commercial men is best proved by the comprehensiveness of the Catalogue of Exhibitors which follows, and the very large number of applications for tickets which have been received. To the Exhibitors who have come here so numerously, and to the Patrons who were the first to countenance the scheme, I am charged by Mr. DALE to offer his heartfelt acknowledgments for their valuable support and encouragement.

D

The Catalogue itself also requires a word or two of introduction. The articles which are printed herewith are an integral portion of the scheme of Trade Exhibitions, and are printed with the object, if possible, of pointing the moral of the present Exhibition, and of offering some useful suggestions and entertaining information to those who may read the work. It is hoped that, by this means, the Catalogue will not be regarded as of so ephemeral a nature as to be worthy of no better fate than that of the waste-paper basket or the butterman ; but that, when a pleasant half-hour with it has induced its reader to place it permanently on his bookshelf, he will keep it long enough to enable him at some future period to recall with interest what were the most approved *impedimenta* of the printer in the year 1880, and what were the most advanced views which at that time prevailed in the Trade. What he may then think of those views I do not know, but, for the present, I am sure he will join with me in thanking the gentlemen who have expounded them, for the valuable articles they have provided.

The " CLASSIFIED GUIDE TO EXHIBITS " is a feature which will be found very useful by visitors whose time is limited, and who wish to inspect only certain kinds of exhibits. Instead of exploring the whole building, or carefully reading through the entire Catalogue, they need only look for the special exhibit, or class of exhibits, in its alphabetical place and its position in the Hall will be immediately ascertained.

LUCIEN WOLF.

AGRICULTURAL HALL,
July 5th, 1880.

C. G. SQUINTANI & CO.'S Exhibit is in the Centre of the Hall, and comprises, besides the "MODEL" Printing Press (see pp. 14 & 154), several Novelties for Printers, Stationers and Bookbinders.

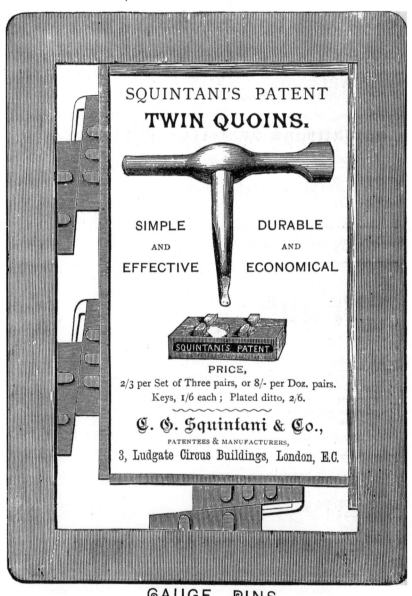

SQUINTANI'S PATENT
TWIN QUOINS.

SIMPLE   DURABLE
AND   AND
EFFECTIVE   ECONOMICAL

PRICE,
2/3 per Set of Three pairs, or 8/- per Doz. pairs.
Keys, 1/6 each ; Plated ditto, 2/6.

C. G. Squintani & Co.,
PATENTEES & MANUFACTURERS,
3, Ludgate Circus Buildings, London, E.C.

GAUGE PINS.

Four for 6d. or 1/- per Dozen.   IMPROVED, Four for 1/- or 2/6 per Dozen.
See also pp. 14 & 154.

THE FUTURE OF TRADE EXHIBITIONS.

By the EDITOR.

THE variety of Exhibitions is now-a-days without end. Almost every thing moveable and concrete, and for the matter of that, even things immoveable and abstract, if we consider the goals of the tourist, and the *séances* of the evolvers of new ideas, is made the subject of some kind of show, and few days of the week pass without the public is invited, through the medium of circulars or the daily papers, to inspect some new aggregation of products or manufactures, some laborious collection of the results of artistic efforts, or of the eccentricities of nature, science, and ingenuity. There are, however, Exhibitions *and* Exhibitions. To the general public this may possibly appear an oracular, not to say, an ambiguous announcement. The "general public" unfortunately has hitherto not regarded Exhibitions in the abstract as worthy objects of exegetical criticism. They have generally paid their shillings and feasted their eyes, and there was an end of their amusement. In a hazy sort of way, a few of them have been aware that, according to some poetical thinkers, Exhibitions are the "Festivals of Peace," and that according to others they are the "Battles of Peace;" they have not been able to reconcile these soaring metaphors, and so they have not thought much more about them. Again they have heard of wild debates between divergent sets of economical thinkers on the disturbing effects of such and such an Exhibition, and of the commercial

advantages of some other great show. The profound problems
of political economy upon which these discussions have been
based have unfortunately rendered them somewhat of the nature
of *caviare* to the vulgar, and so they also have not com-
manded much attention at the hands of the hard-headed
" general public." *Faute de mieux*, what then is the view which
this same " general public " has hitherto held, and still
holds, about exhibitions? It is that they are Shows, *et præteria
nihil* — some amusing, some interesting, but Shows for all
that. A further enquiry into this view will reveal the fact
that this eminently respectable " general public" does not
at all regard this species of Show with aversion. It is as
a moral and educational companion to the Polytechnic and
the Albert Memorial, as a mildly exhilarating reward for much
Sunday School and Tea Meeting attendance, that the modern
Exhibition is regarded by the classes to which I refer, and to
them the " Show," as a rule, is more or less entertaining, in the
same ratio that it is varied and extensive. Now this view of
Shows, as a rule, is by no means an unjust or unnatural one ; and
it is not unnatural, for the simple reason that, of the majority of
Shows, it is perfectly just ; but, as I before remarked, there are
Exhibitions *and* Exhibitions ; and of a certain class of these exhibitions the ·" general public " would be very much in error to
think in the wise I have indicated. The kind of Exhibition to
which I am referring is the Trade Exhibition ; and the reason
that I have spoken of the popular errors which prevail respecting exhibitions generally, is that the Trade Exhibition has
before it at the present moment a very extensive sphere of
utility, and an extremely practical and intelligible mission, in
which all classes of the mercantile community are deeply
interested ; and it is desirable that the " general public," who
constitute the backbone of the mercantile community, should be
enabled to correctly appreciate the *raison d'être*, and the future
of a system which is destined very much to influence their own

material comforts. Whilst these correct estimates remain uninculcated the legitimate development of the Trade Exhibition must be impeded, and although I am not so pretentious as to imagine that from my feeble words is immediately to spring a rehabilitation of ideas on this subject, at least I hope that what may be said by myself and others who think with me, will contribute to the much desired result.

The Trade Exhibition is as little a " show," in the general acceptation of the term, as its organizer is a "showman." In fact, as far as the term " exhibition " itself has become "polarised" by its association with the international *fêtes* which were in-augurated in 1851, it is a misnomer as applied to the Trade Exhibition, for the very simple reason that in its conception, as well as in its realization, it has been altogether different from the International Exhibition. In so far, however, as the terms of its establishment render it necessary that merchandise should be laid out for public inspection, it is a show or an exhibition,—whichever term may suit the reader—but here its identity with other shows and exhibitions altogether ceases. It is neither a museum nor a booth of monstrosities; nor a bazaar, a world fair, a gallery, a " tournament," or a " demonstration." It is in fact *sui generis*, and what is more, of no very ancient origin; it is therefore pardonable that misapprehension as to its aims should prevail. But little enquiry will suffice to show that it is the outcome solely of certain commercial and industrial developments which have rendered some such institution necessary. The want that is supplied by the Trade Exhibition is the opportunity for meeting one another periodically, which the several classes in a large number of trades have long desired. It has been deeply felt for a considerable time that buyers and sellers, wholesalers, retailers, agents and importers should be enabled to meet together on a fairer and a more open basis than is possible under existing systems of trading. Now-a-days, when competition is so bitter, and so much depends upon being able to buy well and cheaply, and to keep oneself *au courant* with the progress of invention, the mercantile and industrial classes are beginning to see that with every enterprise and care they cannot always make sure of doing all this under the present systems of commercial travelling and advertising. They require some common meeting ground, where producers and retailers can meet and take a personal and comprehensive view of the state of their several trades, where they can see not only what their neighbours are manufacturing, and what enterprising geniuses are patenting, but what their most remote competitors are producing, and what the humblest ingenuity is inventing ; where retailers or wholesalers, as the case may be, may compare the products and the prices of a hundred establishments before buying, and where all may have the advertisement they require, at once confined to the very classes to whom they appeal, and limited in its cost. It is this great want, or rather constellation of wants, which Trade Exhibitions have been initiated to supply, and as far as can be gathered as yet, the steps which have been taken to realise this programme have met with perfect satisfaction. I can state from my personal knowledge that the realization of the programme I have mentioned has been Mr. Dale's great idea ever since he conceived last year's National Exhibition and Market, and I cannot help saying—although it is to a certain extent in his presence—that he has taken some very ingenious steps in the prosecution of his idea. In the first place, he has made a point of supplying great manufacturers gratuitously with large numbers of tickets of admission for the use of their workmen. Now this, I think, was a very wise step, for it encourages the manufacturers to let their *employés* learn from the exhibition the same lessons that they themselves may learn—learn how superior is So-and-So's work, or how much cheaper somebody else's productions ; and, if possible, learn the why and the wherefore. In these days of capital and labour disputes there can be no doubt that such practical demonstration to workmen of the real condition of their trades is calculated to do a great deal of good. Another very wise step on the part of Mr. Dale is his offering, under certain conditions, to the trades interested free admission to his exhibitions. This at once reveals the true nature of the Trade Exhibition, for rendering it "free to the trade" really means that it sacrifices a good many shillings, in order to remove every barrier to that free intercourse which is now so much required. This marks in a very broad line the distinction between the Trade Exhibition and the ordinary show. Then, in addition to this, the exhibitors are entitled to any number of invitation tickets, at a nominal cost, for distribution by them amongst people likely to be interested in the exhibits. These three features are, in the history of Exhibitions, thoroughly novel, and their introduction by Mr. Dale has materially contributed to the uniqueness of the Trade Exhibition. There can be but few amongst those who may peruse these remarks who will not agree with me that the Trade Exhibition, with the policy I have described, marks an important—nationally important—departure in the systems of trading of this country.

Like every great movement which may have for its basis legitimate and widely-felt requirements, the Trade Exhibition has in England a great future. The commerce and industry of this country are now in a state of transition; an upheaval is manifesting itself within their particular domains, which seems destined to annihilate all the antique and anachronistic methods to which they are so much a prey. Time was, when it mattered little by what means or methods our trade was carried on. The energy of our industrial and mercantile classes was only equalled by their good luck, and whatever we touched turned literally to gold. Those were, however, ante-telegraphic, ante-railway, and ante-exhibition days; no man troubled himself about his neighbour, and no country

concerned itself in the least about the trade of any other
country. The quiet, imperturbable, and prosperous atmosphere
in which commercial transactions were then conducted, suited
exactly the taste of the English merchant, whose predilections
were all for respectability before enterprise, and dignified
punctuality before bustling activity. In those old days competition was almost unknown, and, indeed, the bare idea of
one tradesman thinking of under-selling another, presupposed
a consciousness of his existence which might almost be called
"forward," and an acquaintance with his affairs which could
only be described as prying curiosity. Thus, every merchant
and every retailer had a little snuggery of his own, with a
range of old customers who were almost like family friends,
and who mutually handed down one another from generation to
generation with a fidelity which rendered their incomes, in each
case, even safer than if derived from Government securities.
These times have, however, changed; but unfortunately it
cannot be said, with the proverb, that in the same ratio *nos
mutamur in illis*. Now, all is competition, and business is
really *business;* but whilst foreign countries have all, according
to their lights, gone with these times, in England the alteration
in the commercial conditions, and in the methods of business,
has not been synchronous. Nor is the reason far to seek. In
that Golden Age of semi-somnolent prosperity, that Cheeryble
period of commercial morality which, I fear, is gone from us
for ever, both fortunes and competencies were made so surely,
so easily, and on so conservative a basis, that it would
be almost supernatural to expect a ready and cheerful compliance with that new law of modern trading which prescribes
a much larger amount of work at a much lower rate of pay.
And in England this compliance with the new *Weltwirthschaft*
has been longer and more stubbornly withheld, because the anti-
thetical conditions of former years flourished here more luxu-
riantly than in any country. But what have been the results?

Whilst abroad, and in the New World, trade has, on the whole
been active, in consequence of the systematic manner in which
it has been conducted; in England we have experienced an
unexampled succession of depressed periods, arising in a great
measure out of our reluctance to acquiesce in the times—a reluctance which has been dictated by a blind refusal to believe in
the reality of Yankee go-a-headedness. As, however, water
cannot drip persistently upon a rock without making a lasting
impression, and without ultimately altering its shape, so, also, as
period after period of commercial stagnation has developed itself
in this country, wonder and indignation have given way to
anxiety, anxiety has generated inquiry, and inquiry is now
developing into conversion. Thus it is that our trade is now
going through a transition state, and gradually, as we are forced
to acknowledge that this and that device of modern economy is,
under the new conditions, necessary to our well-being, we are
acclimatizing it and adapting ourselves to it. Look wherever
we may, and signs of this reversal of policy meet our gaze.
There never was a period in our history when all classes of men
took so profound an interest in statistical and economical studies.
Mechanics' institutes, and debating societies, working men's
clubs, and ordinary reading rooms, are now every day occupied
by disputants, whose enquiries are all directed to the solution of
the problem, " What further resources are possessed by science
for the improvement of our material interests ? " The masters
and workmen, who were once like the happy family of Arcadian
romance, are now divided into two vast camps, severally called
Trades Unions and Federations of Employers of Labour ; and,
much as we may deplore the strife which so often occupies their
energies, we cannot but recognise that they owe their existence
to the popular discovery of a very great and valuable principle
—the principle of combined organization and association. Then,
again, the debates which agitate the country on such questions
as the Land Laws, or the respective merits of free trade and

protective policies, and the necessity of a special Ministry of Commerce and Agriculture, are pregnant indications of an anxious tendency to commercial reform. Another example may be found in the cry which has gone up from every manufacturing district and every mercantile centre for technical education on a large and comprehensive scale. There was a time when education was looked upon as the pre-ordained monopoly of the few, and everything but the teachings of a mechanical apprenticeship was jealously withheld from the working man ; now we see all classes combining for his scientific instruction. Technical schools and technical museums are being established everywhere, and whilst they receive ready and handsome subventions from masters, they are largely attended by artisans. This is the transforming machinery which is now happily at work in our commercial systems ; the Trade Exhibition is the latest, but by no means the least important, engine of this class which has been introduced.

With the programme before it which I have described, and established under the changing conditions upon which we all felicitate ourselves, the Trade Exhibition should be, and I believe is, destined to play a part of no mean consequence in the commercial future of this country. Notwithstanding. the vastness of the schemes of transformation which are now before us, there is yet much which would have to be effected by means of the Trade Exhibition. To the inventor especially it is brimful of promise. What with the sharpening of the natural capacities of our workmen by the friction of harder conditions of life, and the improved systems of technical education of which they may now avail themselves, I believe we are on the threshold of a period of small inventors. Now, in the present condition of our Patent Law, how are these small inventors to protect themselves and to reap the benefit of their ingenuity ? If we consult any antiquated economical authority we shall find that the idea which prompted the institution of Patent protection was the

development of invention. In point of fact, however, the
Patent protection of the present day has quite the opposite
effect. It discourages invention instead of stimulating it, for
the protection it offers is so expensive that only the rich
can avail themselves of it, and even they very often find
themselves so handicapped by this expense and the general
unsympathetic tendency of the law, that when their term
of protection has expired they find they have not reaped
a reward commensurate with the benefits they may have
conferred on their species. Now for all inventors alike, but
especially for the small, or rather, poor inventor, the Trade
Exhibition will be a very great encouragement. In the first
place, by the operation of the "Protection of Inventions Act,
1870," exhibitors of new inventions are guaranteed by the Board
of Trade, without any further form or cost, a protection equal to
Provisional Protection. This is a very great advantage, for
whilst the price which the exhibitor pays for his place at such
an exhibition would, if he were economical, be considerably
less than what he would pay for provisional protection, at the
same time—provided always that the exhibition is a *Trade*
Exhibition, and limited in its scope—he would bring his invention
under the prominent notice of the very people to whom he would
wish to address himself, but who, under other circumstances,
he could only reach with very great difficulty, and collectively not
at all. Thus exhibited, the merits of a new invention could not
fail to to be accurately gauged, and the inventor to be adequately
remunerated for his labour and ingenuity. It is in fact like
a lowering of the Patent charges, and an extension of Society of
Arts' conferences rolled into one. Untold advantages have been
prophesied from a diminution of the Southampton Buildings
tariff; what may not be anticipated from the combination of
advantages which, under this heading, will be provided by Trade
Exhibitions? Some of our greatest inventors have sprung from
the working classes, and who knows how many Stephensons

and Arkwrights may yet be developed from the *residuum* by the easy terms I have described.

This is, however, not all that the Trade Exhibition aims at doing. I do not know whether I am an enthusiast, but I think that the mental survey which any one who studies the subject may make of its future is, I will not say far too great to grapple with, but far too multifarious to permit of its being described with a due regard for the patience of the reader. I may, however, point out that, when Trade Exhibitions are properly developed in accordance with the exigencies of the trades for whose benefits they are held, they will gradually build up and perfect a much fairer system of business than at present prevails. I do not think that I speak unpractically when I say that, much as the competition of modern trading may have done for the consumer, its benefits are susceptible of a very heavy discount when it is considered how very generally in the bitterness of the strife such weapons as chicanery and mendacity are freely used. And they are used, too, with impunity, for under existing circumstances, trade is conducted with very many persons in the dark. In those departments where markets do not exist, and prices are not a matter of every-day regulation, goods are bought and sold with but very little real knowledge of the immediate present or the immediate future of such trades ; no opportunities exist for the simultaneous comparison of the products of different manufacturers, and few people buy with a thorough knowledge of how well they could buy. Even the best of business men can but have a very imperfect understanding on this head, and thus it is that, as a good deal of trade is transacted by means of the personal recommendation and persuasion of commercial travellers, much is sold that ought never to be brought on the market, and much is bought that is not at all wanted. If the Trade Exhibitions are timed for the buying seasons all this would be altered, and indeed Mr. Dale has informed me that for both his recent exhibitions buyers so far recognised their advantages that they purposely postponed their usual purchases in order to be able to buy with their eyes wide open at the Agricultural Hall. Then, again, the Trade Exhibition as a means of advertising is far more moral than newspaper advertising. The large majority of the advertisements which are printed together with our periodical literature are designedly drawn up for the entrapment of the unwary, and this is further aggravated by the puffery which may very often be easily purchased. Specialities and novelties exhibited at a Trade Exhibition can deceive no one, for their puffery cannot be anything more deceptive than a shopman's pursuasive eloquence, and the least 'cute of business men are very apt to allow what they see to outweigh what they hear.

Many other potentialities of the trade exhibition will readily occur to the reader without any further suggestion from me. That its future is one of great promise cannot for a moment be doubted, for it must have an educational effect upon all classes; it will undoubtedly offer very substantial encouragement to the inventor, and upon trade generally its moral influence will be very powerful. I may add, that in order still more to promote that *entente cordiale*, and the development of that "multitude of council" in which we are assured "is wisdom," Mr. Dale intends, in any of his future exhibitions where such a thing may be required, to hold a Conference in connection with the exhibition, at which papers may be read, and discussions take place, on questions of importance to the trades interested.

THE ORIGIN AND PROGRESS OF PRINTING.

BY JOHN SOUTHWARD.

THE Catalogue of the "Exhibition and Mart of Machinery, Implements and Material used or sold by Printers and kindred Traders," need not be prefaced by any definition of Printing. This is fortunate; for no complete or precise definition of the art has yet been given. All the definitions of the lexicographers and the encyclopædias will be found to be faulty, if carefully examined in the light which a practical knowledge of the art throws upon the subject. Some are too comprehensive, and would include every image or facsimile obtained by mere pressure, like stamped clay bricks, coins, and seals; others are too exclusive, and leave out prints from plain surfaces, like lithographs, and from photographic negatives, both of which are largely utilised for literary as well as graphic purposes.

In regard to the *utility* of the art there can be no possible difference of opinion. It has effected a greater influence upon mankind than any other mechanical invention; and has diffused religion, arts, commerce, and civilisation to a larger extent than the most enthusiastic of philosophers could possibly have anticipated. "Until printing was generally spread," says Babbage, in one of the Bridgewater Treatises, "civilisation advanced by slow and languid steps; since that art has become cheap, its advances have become unparalleled, and its rate of progress vastly accelerated. It has been stated by some that the civilisation of the Western World has resulted from its being the seat of the Christian religion. However much the mild tenour of its doctrines is calculated to assist in producing such an effect, that religion can but be injured by an unfounded

E

statement. It is the easy and chief methods of communicating thought from man to man which enable a country to sift, as it were, its whole people, and to produce in its science, its literature, and its arts, not the brightest efforts of a limited class, but the highest exertions of the most powerful minds among a whole community—it is this which has given birth to the wide-spreading civilisation of the present day, and which promises a futurity yet more prolific. Whoever is acquainted with the present state of science and the mechanical arts, and looks back over the inventions and civilisation which the fourteen centuries, subsequent to the introduction of Christianity have produced, and compares them with the advances made during the succeeding four centuries following the invention of Printing, will have no doubt as to the effective cause. It is during these last three or four centuries that man, considered as a species, has commenced the development of his intellectual faculties, that he has emerged from a position in which he was almost the creature of instinct, to a state in which every step in advance facilitates the progress of his successors. In the first period arts were discovered by individuals and lost to the race ; in the latter the diffusion of ideas enabled the reasoning of one class to unite with the observation of another, and the most advanced point of one generation becomes the starting-post of the next."

Who invented printing ? The simple answer is, no one knows. The "art preservative of all arts" to quote the tablet in front of the alleged Koster House at Haarlem, has not preserved the secret of its own origin. This may appear a hazardous assertion, to those who thought that the controversy on the subject had been settled by the researches, published ten years ago, of Dr. Van der Linde ; and are not aware that one of our most learned bibliographers is at this moment engaged in a microscopic examination of the Dutch doctor's proofs of the German invention of typography ; and that the rival claims of Holland may be very strongly strengthened by the results of this examination. A list of the books which have been written on this one question would extend, perhaps, to three thousand numbers; and the period during which the controversy has been waged extends from 1561 to 1880.

Whether the art of typography was invented in the Low Countries or in Germany is, therefore, still an open question; and it will probably ever remain so, for most of the original documents, forming evidence which should influence the decision of the historian, were, most unhappily, destroyed in the burning of the Strasburg Library during the recent Franco-Prussian war. There is little doubt, however, that one original and independent inventor of the art was John Gutenberg; and that to his press at Mayence may be traced the beginning of an art subsequently disseminated throughout the whole civilised world.

Little space must be allotted here to an account of this remarkable man. There is no record of his birth; but it is believed he was born at Mayence about the year 1397. His parents were Frielo Gensfleisch and Else Gutenberg, and he took his mother's patronymic. Except what is known as to a casual visit to Mayence, the first thirty years of his life are a complete blank; and little would be known concerning his subsequent career but for the circumstance that he was compelled on several occasions to make appearances in law courts, and give some sort of account of himself. There are records of his suing and being sued; and of his having been defendant in a " breach of promise of marriage " case; and that is about all we know of him with certainty. He appears to have been a man of a mechanical turn of mind, and to have been experimenting in the art of type-founding about the year 1439, in profound secrecy, but associated for financial reasons with a kind of syndicate of moneyed persons. In 1450, after his partnership had been dissolved, and the whole of his funds were expended, he went to a professional money-lender of Mayence, named John Fust, and borrowed a sum of money for the purpose of printing an edition of the great Bible. About 1456 two different editions of the holy books were completed; copies are preserved, the editions being known respectively as the Gutenberg or " 42 line Bible," and the Bamberg or " 36 line Bible." In 1873 a copy, on vellum, of the first-named was sold at auction in London for £3,400, and one on paper for £2,900. On their first issue, however, the publication was unsuccessful; Gutenberg could not repay the money he had borrowed, and the lender, Fust, took possession of his type and presses.

Gutenberg at this time must have been about sixty years old, but he had sufficient energy left to start a new office. He was able to borrow more money, some of his old workmen stood by him, and in 1460 he completed a book called " The Catholicon," a combination of a Latin grammar and dictionary. In 1465 he was raised to an office somehow connected with the Court, and most probably retired from business. It is not even known when he died, but he was dead in 1468.

These details may seem very bare ; and so they undoubtedly are. The writer of this has spent years in the study of the history of typography, and has consulted some hundreds of the works that have been written on the subject ; yet the above are nearly all the facts that he can give with confidence.

John Fust carried on printing in conjunction with one Peter Schoeffer, a young man of about 26 years of age, who was employed in Gutenberg's office, and who ultimately became Fust's son-in-law. There are a lot of romantic stories extant about his caligraphy, and his proficiency in punch-cutting ; they are nearly all baseless. In 1457 the two printed a Psalter. This, as well as Gutenberg's bibles, is a splendid book, and a truly marvellous production for the infancy of printing. There are copies of the three in the British Museum

In 1462, it should be stated, the city of Mayence was besieged and captured. The workmen employed by the three earliest printers were dispersed, and carried the knowledge of the art into different countries ; new offices were founded, but is unfortunate that not one of their owners has told us when, and how, he began to print on his own account. In short, the early history of the art is most distressingly obscure. Superficial and credulous, and especially non-practical writers, have given us copious accounts of the invention and the spread of printing, but the more thoroughly their statements are examined, the less residuum of truth is found to be at the bottom of them. We have, in nearly every instance, to fix the year of printing being introduced into the various countries according to dates which books may have borne.

The first book printed in the English language was the "Recuyell of the Histories of Troye'; a large volume containing 351 leaves. It does not state when or where or by whom it was printed. Hence controversy has arisen on this point; but the best, indeed, perhaps, the only authority on the subject, Mr. William Blades, states that it was printed at Bruges by one Colard Mansion and William Caxton about 1474. It was during the printing of this book, as Caxton tells us, that he learnt his new art.

The first book printed in England was "The Dictes and notable wise Sayings of the Philosophers," and there is a definite statement that it was "Emprynted by me, Wylliam Caxton, at Westminstre, 1477."

It is not our intention, however, to write a sketch of the history of Printing. All that we can do, within the very limited space at our disposal, is to present a few leading dates, and to enumerate the chief improvements in processes, machinery, and materials achieved within certain intervals.

THE PRINTING PRESS.

THE earliest pictorial representation of a printing press is one that dates back to 1507. It is a woodcut, used as a device on the title-page of a book printed by Jodocus Badius Ascensius, the celebrated printer of Paris. We do not know what kind of a press Gutenberg used; probably it was an apparatus something like a clothes press, with a platen made to approach the bed by the use of a screw. The press was not the essence of Gutenberg's invention; it was the method of casting moveable type.

In this first press of which we have any trustworthy account all the elements of modern presses are to be found. The type forme is laid upon a bed, which is brought under the platen by means of a travelling carriage and rounce. There is a tympan and a frisket. The platen, however, was so small that almost every forme must have required two pulls. This was owing to the nature of the mechanism—a flat plane, of hard material, moved parallel to itself, brought to press on a forme of type laid upon a hard surface parallel to the moving plane. This involves two difficulties; the distribution of the pressure from a central suspension, and the preservation of the parallelism of the moving plane with the type.

This press was in general use for nearly three centuries. The first improvement of which we have any account was made in Amsterdam, about the middle of the 17th century, either by Nicholas Blaew, or by his son William Jansen Blaew, who rendered the platen more free from lateral deflection, and added a contrivance whereby the platen raised itself when the bar was returned to its place. Printers did not at first appreciate these innovations; Moxon, the first English writer on practical printing (1683), describes Blaew's as a "new fashioned press," and recommends it. When, however, its advantages were acknowledged it was adopted as the universal model, and so remained till the beginning of the present century.

The first really great improver of the printing press was Charles Mahon, third Earl of Stanhope. He abandoned the straight bar and screw of the old wooden press and adopted a system of links and levers. The approach and withdrawal of the platen were thus rendered more rapid, and the fullest amount of pressure was obtained just at the right moment. Above all, the press was made entirely of iron; previous ones had been almost wholly of wood, except the screw, the bed, and less important parts. They were thus cumbrous, and could not bear heavy strains. Stanhope was able to use a platen of double the ordinary size.

This improved press was never patented, and all press-makers were therefore free to copy its improvements. They largely availed themselves of the privilege granted by the patriotic earl. In 1813, John Ruthven, of Edinburgh, made other improvements, one of which was causing the Stanhope

lever to act direct upon the margins of the platen and not at
the centre, as had been the custom previously. He placed the
heavy and moving parts as near the base as possible, and thus
gained stability, and provided for a ready and accurate adjustment of the parellelism of the platen with the type. Thomas
Cogger also introduced improvements; but the two presses
were destined to be eclipsed altogether by an American invention, the now well-known "Columbian Press."

George Clymer came over to England from Philadelphia,
and, in 1817, patented his "Columbian Press." He gave
greater efficiency and range to the bar, and increased strength
to the essential parts of the press. The platen was attached to
a powerful lever by means of a square bar working in guides.
The object of the heavy eagle ornament on the head was to
secure the self-acting recovery of the platen.

In 1824, Mr. R. W. Cope devised the well-known Albion
Press. The Stanhope system of lever was retained. In the
Columbian this principle is applied by means of links and pin-
points; in the Albion by means of surfaced V plates of steel.

These two inventions still remain in favor wherever hand
presses are used. Excepting the very large sizes, the Albion
has, probably, been preferred, but for heavy work the Columbian
is perhaps the most useful.

We must now refer to the Printing Machine, which has
nearly superseded hand presses. In 1790, one of the most
extraordinary patents on record was taken out by William
Nicholson. It included almost every improvement which the
last ninety years has seen adopted; yet it was impracticable,
and no machine was ever built according to the specification·
Nicholson's object was to make an apparatus which should print
almost automatically; and he discarded the platen in favour
of a cylinder, as the pressing surface. In Nicholson's patent
is included a travelling type bed, a roller for distributing and
applying the ink, and grippers for seizing the sheet of paper
to be printed. He even anticipated the quite recently adopted
system of printing from reels of paper. Where Nicholson
failed was in not being able to curve his printing surface round
a cylinder; had he known how to cast a plate, and to bend it

to the necessary shape, or even to fasten the type by the method afterwards devised by Hoe, he would have been the first practical inventor of the printing machine.   That distinction, however, was to be conferred upon Frederick Koenig, a Saxon, who, while working as a printer at Leipzig, was impressed with the idea that the operations of printing might be simplified and accelerated.   He received no encouragement in Germany, and came to London in 1806.   Mr. Thomas Bensley, the well-known printer, provided him with funds to work out his scheme, and Mr. George Woodfall and Mr. Richard Taylor afterwards joined the partnership.   With the mechanical assistance of a friend Mr. A. Bauer, Koenig made, in 1810, a platen machine, on which, in 1811, was printed the first sheet of a book ever worked " on machine."

It is not on record whether Koenig was cognisant of Nicholson's proposals.   In 1812, however, he produced a machine in which the previous inventor's principle of a cylinder and a travelling type-bed was adopted.   Two sheets of a book were printed on this in December, 1812.   The remarkable character of the invention reaching the ears of Mr. John Walter, of *The Times*, he went to see it, and forthwith ordered a machine to print his newspaper.   It was a two-feeder machine, driven by steam power, turning out about 1,000 impressions per hour. It was first actually used for the production of an entire issue of the journal, 29th November, 1814.

About this time, Donkin and Bacon were also experimenting on printing machinery, and took out a patent for an apparatus in which the types were placed on a revolving prism, the ink being applied by a roller which rose and fell in accordance with the irregularities of the prism.   The sheet to be printed was carried on to another prism, so formed as to meet the irregularities of the type prism.   The machine, after a few trials, was found to be too complicated, and never came into actual use.

In 1816, Koenig patented a perfecting machine, and afterwards otherwise improved *The Times* machine, so that the proprietor was enabled to turn out about 2,000 impressions per hour.

The two next improvers of the printing machine were

Augustus Applegath and Edward Cowper. They greatly simplified and improved the existing model, and, in 1824, invented the perfecting machine, which, in its principal features, is still in use in book printing offices. In 1827, they constructed a four-cylinder machine, which printed 6,000 impressions per hour, and completely superseded Koenig's. It remained in use until 1848, when Applegath devised another machine on quite a novel principle. There were eight impression cylinders which revolved on vertical axes, the type being affixed to a large rotary cylinder. By this means about 12,000 impressions per hour were produced.

Applegath's machine was adopted at *The Times* office until the advent of an American invention of remarkable ingenuity. This was a machine built by Mr. R. M. Hoe, of New York, and it was not only more compact than the Applegath, but could be driven at a higher rate of speed. The first machine of the kind was fitted up at the office of *Lloyd's News*, in 1857. The cylinders were horizontal, there being from two to ten impression cylinders, the latter giving nearly 20,000 impressions per hour. One remarkable feature of the Hoe machines was that the takers-off were dispensed with, by the invention of "flyers." Moveable type was used, and it was very ingeniously arranged on the large cylinder. Each column of type was set upon the level, but six or seven columns, for a large newspaper, were nevertheless adjusted side by side. Brass rules of a bevelled shape were placed between the columns, the bevel varying according to the curvature of the cylinder. All the columns of type were then adjusted and tightened up, to occupy, in polygonal fashion, a portion of the circumference of the cylinder, the remaining portion affording space for the inking rollers to act. At a later date, stereotype plates, each strictly conforming to the curvature of the cylinder, were introduced, with a great increase of speed and economy. By increasing the diameter of the cylinder, room was found for an increased number of pressure cylinders around it, insomuch that, as already stated, there were machines with two, four, six, eight, and ten pressing cylinders, printing an equal number of sheets during one revolution of the main cylinder.

In 1868 a new and remarkable machine was imported from France by the proprietor of the *London Echo*, a four-page evening paper. It was the invention of M. Hippolyte Marinoni, of Paris, and was a rotary six-feeder perfecting machine, in which it differed from all previous machines, as they worked one side only. The stereotype plates were arranged on the surfaces of two rotating cylinders, the sheets of paper being fed in by six layers-on, at six different positions on the machine. The *Echo* being only half the size of the ordinary morning journals, 20,000 copies were printed per hour, there being two copies on one sheet, which was afterwards severed. The pressure cylinder and the tapes were so nicely adjusted that the sheets, fed by the six layers-on, followed in an almost continuous stream, only about an inch apart. After the sheets passed over and under the printing cylinder, they were divided by tapes into two streams, one passing to the right and the other to the left; each of these again was divided into an upper and lower stream, and the four streams of sheets were deposited by hinged flyers on four receiving tables, whence they were removed at intervals in large piles. The cutting was done by a rotating circular knife, parallel to the medial line of the machine. The sheets were deposited on the receiving tables by flyers.

In 1862 the proprietors of *The Times* commenced experiments, having two main objects in view—to print from a continuous roll of paper instead of single sheets, and to print both sides at once. Those who were chiefly engaged on the experiments were Mr. John Walter, chief proprietor; Mr. J. C. Macdonald, manager; and Mr. J. Calverley, chief engineer of the establishment. So new were the combinations of parts, that the tools for making them were themselves made on *The Times* premises; and a large machine shop produced both the tools and the machines. The co-operation of paper-makers, ink-makers, and stereotypers was necessary. A web of paper was wanted sufficiently wide to make two pages of *The Times*; sufficiently strong to bear winding on the reel, printing on the machine, and cutting afterwards. The curvilinear plates had to be perfectly true or they would not give a good impression. Apparatus for damping the paper, cutting it, counting it, and delivering it were also required. Perfect register was necessary, and a speed was aimed at of from 12,000 to 16,000 complete sheets per hour.

The experiments were carried on during the six years between 1862 and 1868, and at last one machine was finished. Three more were then begun, and these were completed by the end of 1869, when the edition of *The Times* was printed on them in less than half the time previously occupied, and with one-fifth of the hands required for the Hoe machines, besides the great saving effected by reducing the number of inking rollers and blankets, the smaller quantity of ink used, and a much less waste of paper.

In the Walter machine a web of paper was used, weighing about six cwt., and uncoiling to the length of about four miles. The web or roll was adjusted at one end of the machine, and when exhausted was replaced by another, with a delay of little more than a minute. The paper travelled through the machine at an average rate of about 1,000ft. per minute, so that a roll was exhausted in less than half-an-hour. The paper was led from the reel to a series of small cylinders, supplied with water so as to damp it. It then approached a range of four larger cylinders placed one over the other, the uppermost being encircled by the stereotype plates for four pages, or one side of the newspaper; the lowermost by those for the four pages of the other side; while the second and third were pressure cylinders. The paper was printed on one side while passing between the first and second cylinders, and on the other while passing between the third and fourth. The inking was managed by reservoirs and rollers near the cylinders. The printed paper then encountered a beautiful apparatus which cut up the continuous web into separate sheets. One of two cylinders had a groove along the top; another, over and in contact with it, had a knife along the bottom; a brass guard flanked this knife in such a way as to cause it to protrude and recede alternately; the protrusion of the knife cutting the paper at rigorously equal intervals. The knife was not a smooth edge; it made a row of perforations almost close together, and the paper was pulled asunder at the next onward movement. An index hand, connected with the cutting cylinders, recorded the number of sheets cut. The sheets following in a close stream, were led up by a set of tapes to the highest part of the machine; from this point they descended perpendicularly, and were thrown alternately backwards and forwards, by an oscillating tape-frame, on two delivery tables, whence they were removed at intervals in large piles. The machine pumped up its own ink from a tank beneath the floor, preparatory to the distribution by the inking rollers. Only three men were required in the actual working: one to start and stop the machine, and two to attend to the delivery of the sheets; no layers-on were needed. In all machines which printed separated sheets, the speed of working depended mainly on the speed of laying-on; and as there is a limit to the nimbleness of human hands in this work, the only means of increasing the rate of printing is by duplicating or multiplying the number of impression cylinders for each type-bearing or stereotype-bearing surface; when these impression cylinders exceed six in number the complication becomes great, the stoppages frequent, the waste considerable, the risk of accidents serious, and the cost of the work heavy; hence the advantage of printing a continuous roll, and separating the sheets after printing.

Several improvements have since been introduced into *The Times* machine, adapting it for printing thinner paper than that used for "the leading journal," and it is now used by various other newspapers.

The web principle is evidently the one on which all largely circulated papers will be printed in the future. The merit of having first completed a practical Rotary web printing machine is due to William Bullock, an engineer of Philadelphia, U.S.A., whose first press was finished in 1865, after years of patient experiment. The inventor did not long enjoy the fruits of his labours, for he was accidentally killed while testing one of his machines, in 1868. The patents afterwards passed into the hands of a company, who supplied the London *Daily Telegraph* with a machine which was at work even before the Walter press.

Some time before 1869, Mr. George Wilson and Mr. George Duncan, of Liverpool, jointly invented the "Victory" machine, and in 1870, a ·year after the first machine was constructed, added apparatus for folding. The machine is now manufactured by a limited liability company, at Liverpool. Each machine prints, folds, and delivers, from 10,000 ,to 12,000 copies of an eight-page paper per hour. Messrs. Bond and Foster, of Preston, have invented a web machine to print from moveable type. The Hoe and the Marinoni machines have been modified to work from the reel. Messrs. Dawson, of Otley, are also now manufacturing a machine on this principle. Several other engineers, in different parts of the country, are likewise producing Rotary web machines. At the Paris Exhibition of 1878 the proprietors of the *Illustrated London News* exhibited the first web machine for printing engravings from circular formes on the Rotary principle. It was invented by Mr. William James Ingram, proprietor and son of the founder of that journal; Mr. Brister, the manager of the machine department in that office, having practically carried out his designs.

Thus far we have referred only to large machines, intended for printing newspapers at the highest attainable rate of speed. We have now to speak of what are called "book and jobbing machines," such as are used in the general offices throughout the country. Soon after Cowper and Applegath brought out their first machine, Mr. David Napier invented one that was more compact, and instead of tapes being used, grippers were employed. In 1824 he built one for Thomas Curson Hansard called the "Desideratum," and this machine obtained great favour, and was widely used for nearly 30 years. It had a large impression cylinder, the sheets being fed in from the top.

It seems now almost incredible that, previous to 1850, no jobbing machine proper had been introduced in the Trade—placards, hand-bills, catalogues, and the like had to be either worked on Napier's "Desideratum," or at press. Those machines being designed more particularly for news and book-work were but imperfectly suited for job-work. At this time Mr. Thomas Main was the machine overseer at the *Morning Chronicle* office, and he applied himself to constructing a jobbing machine, one which was not only adapted from its rapidity to newspaper work, but equally well suited, from its comparative cheapness and utility, as well as superiority and non-liability to slur, to every kind of jobbing printing.

Mr. Main commenced manufacturing his machines on his own account, and set up workshops for that purpose. This was his great mistake; he got into difficulties and went to Australia, but had not been located in that colony more than nine months before he fell suddenly dead in the streets of Melbourne. He had, however, introduced a great—indeed a vast—improvement into the appliances of letterpress printing, and others were soon found to carry on the work. He adopted a small cylinder, to which he gave a tumbling motion, which secured great speed. This was greatly improved by Mr. William Conisbee, of Southwark, and has ever since deservedly attained great favour among printers.

After this inventor came Stephen Soulby, an Ulverston newspaper proprietor, and a man of much ingenuity. He brought out a machine called the " Ulverstonian," in which the impression cylinder travelled, instead of the table, which was stationary. It did excellent work, giving a fine, sharp impression, and is even now used in country offices for book headings and general light work. Happening to be at Carlisle, Mr. Soulby encountered Mr. Samuel Bremner, then the manager of Hudson Scott's large printing works, and the late Mr. Joseph M. Powell, then a traveller for type, ink, &c. These two experienced printers induced Soulby to get his machines manufactured at Otley, and this laid the foundation of the vast businesses now carried on there. The first " Ulverstonian " had been made at the Barrow Iron Works, Ulverston, and subsequent machines by Messrs. John Blaylock and Co., of Carlisle. But the defective principle of Soulby's " Ulverstonian " soon became apparent, and it was shortly after superseded by the " Belle Sauvage."

Mr. Bremner shortly after removed to London, and accepted a leading position under the firm of Cassell, Petter and Galpin, La Belle Sauvage Yard. Being a practical mechanic as well as a printer, he took up the subject of jobbing machines, and pro-

duced the " Belle Sauvage " model. The machines were manufactured for Messrs. Cassell and Co. in large numbers, and the
name " Belle Sauvage " became as familiar to printers as that
of " Stanhope " had been half-a-century previously. After a
few years, Mr. Bremner was induced to undertake the management of Messrs. Harrild's works in London. He continued to
make a variety of improvements, and devised the series of
machines now known as " The Bremner."

Concerning the large number of jobbing machines now
manufactured, it may be stated that the large cylinder "Caxton"
machine of Mr. Myers of Southampton was brought out in
1854. Mr. Duncan of Liverpool, in conjunction with Mr.
Boyd, introduced their stopping cylinder machine about 1855.
Henry Ingle's machine was first manufactured in 1858 ; it was
known as the " Sector." In 1861 it was modified, and called
the " City " printing machine.

The now celebrated " Wharfedale " machines—so named
from the little river, the Wharfe, which runs through Otley,
—were originally manufactured by Mr. William Dawson,
who, as stated above, had been making Stephen Soulby's
" Ulverstonian." Their principle was invented by his
foreman, David Payne, a practical engineer of great skill, who
ultimately started a factory of his own, and now competes with
the old firm of William Dawson and Sons in the manufacture
of these beautiful machines. The " Wharfedale " principle is
introduced into the machines of many other makers, among
them being Messrs. Fieldhouse, Elliott & Co., and Messrs.
Watkinson, Otley ; Mr. William Conisbee, Southwark, &c.

The origin of the small jobbing treadle machines may be
traced back to the specification of John Kitchen, of Newcastle,
who, in 1833, patented a "novel arrangement of the several parts
and appendages of a machine for printing from type." In this
invention the printing surface was vertical, and it was inked by
an elastic roller passed up and down. The platen, with the
tympan and frisket, was brought in contact with the forme
by vibrating upon pivots, and fell back for the removal of the
printed sheet and for the supply of a fresh one. We are not
aware whether any machines were constructed according to this
patent.

Mr. George P. Gordon, of New York, a printer endowed with a mechanical turn of mind, and the patentee of a great number of inventions connected with printing machinery, was, however, the first to manufacture a press of the kind, and was the inventor of the annular disc for the distribution of the ink. His machines were known in America as the "Franklin Presses." They were introduced into this country in 1867, by Messrs. Cropper, of Nottingham, under the name of the "Minerva" machines.

The principal competitor with the "Minerva" was the "Liberty," an American machine invented by Mr. F. O. Degener, of New York, who was for some time associated with Mr. Gordon. Since then the "Universal" has come into great favour. It was invented by Merritt Gally, of New York, a dissenting minister. Mr. Kritch, his foreman, has since improved upon it, and now superintends the manufacture of the "Sun" machine, at the works of Messrs. Greenwood and Batley, Leeds.

Other improvements have been made in this class of machinery—by Mr. William Conisbee, in the "Atlas"; Mr. Samuel Bremner, in the "Bremner Treadle"; Mr. Josiah Wade, in the "Arab"; and others.

COMPOSITION ROLLERS.

For about three centuries after the invention of printing, the formes were inked by leather balls. Earl Stanhope made experiments to obtain a suitable roller, and tried skins, silk and other material without success. Then Bryan Donkin hit upon the mixture of glue and treacle in 1811, for the purposes of his polygonal machine, already mentioned. These rollers, however, did not come into use. In 1818 Cowper invented the modern ink table and press roller. Great opposition was at first raised to the innovation, on the part of the press-men, but chiefly through the perseverance of Mr. Robert Harrild, founder of the present great firm of Harrild and Sons, the rollers were gradually introduced, and ultimately altogether superseded the "pelt" balls. Messrs. Harrild made several important improve-ments in the composition. A few years ago glycerine was introduced from America, and is now largely adopted. Many experiments have been made with india-rubber, but the credit of first making a really useful roller of this material is due to Mr. Robert Lanham, a printer. The rollers of many of the fast rotary machines are now made of india-rubber, as also are hand rollers; indeed the supremacy of the glue and treacle mixture is now very seriously threatened.

MOTORS.

THE first printing machine ever driven by steam-power was that of Koenig, constructed for *The Times*, and which commenced to work the impression of that journal in November, 1814. Since that time various motors have been adopted; and, indeed, the vast majority of machines at the present day are driven otherwise than by manual labour. The chief agents used are steam, gas, and water. Up to within the last ten years almost, steam alone was used, but gas-engines are now very largely em-ployed, and to some extent threaten to supersede steam, except where very high powers are required. The form of gas-engine chiefly used by printers is called the "Otto Silent Gas-Engine," made under patents taken out in 1876 and 1877, and of these about 2,000 have been manufactured; but not of course entirely for the use of printers. Messrs. Crossley and Co. of Manchester, the patentees and manufacturers, were the first to introduce into this country a gas-engine, invented by Otto and Langen of Cologne. Previously there had been various engines using gas sold in England, but they were comparative failures. Hence when the Otto and Langen type made its appearance, it was discredited by the previous reputation of this kind of motors. Messrs. Crossley had to contend against this, but their improve-ments were so manifest, that in the sequel upwards of 4,000 engines of this first construction were sold. There were, how-ever, remaining some defects; the patterns were then entirely remodelled, and an engine produced of the horizontal form (previous engines had been upright or vertical), and in which the noisiness of the old pattern was minimised. These engines are guaranteed not to cost more than one penny per hour for gas for each horse-power indicated. They are now made from ½-horse to 40-horse-power indicated.

Messrs. H. S. Cropper and Co. of Nottingham, the makers of the " Minerva " machine, have also invented a gas-engine made from ½-horse-power to 3-horse-power, which is recommended as possessing advantages over steam when a limited amount of power is required, and where the nature of the machinery to be driven is such as to demand motive power during irregular intervals only. Messrs. L. Simon and Sons, of the same town, have produced a gas-engine.

The " Bisschop " Gas-Engine was invented by M. Bisschop, a Parisian engineer, and first shown at the last Paris Exhibition. The patent rights for this and some other countries were purchased by Mr. J. E. H. Andrew, of Stockport. It is made of "one-man-power" (equal to ⅛th h.-p.) upwards. It is very simple in construction, occupies little space, and requires no water. The cost of working the small size is said to be only one halfpenny per hour.

Water motors are in use in some country printing offices, but their general adoption is restricted by the policy of local water companies. A special water-meter is generally required, involving expense both in fixing and in periodical examination; and the motor can only be made available in places where there is a constant supply of water at a certain degree of pressure.

TYPE-FOUNDING.

It is remarkable that so few houses are engaged in this business, as it is highly lucrative, and capable of great development in this country. Five great firms divide among themselves the patronage of nine-tenths of the printers of the present day. They are known as the " Associated Founders," because they belong to a kind of trade union, whose object is to keep up an

uniform scale of prices, and repress competition among their
own body. These great establishments are Caslon and Co.,
Stephenson, Blake and Co., V. and J. Figgins, Sir Charles Reed
and Sons, and Miller and Richard. The origin of all of them
may be traced to the foundry of the first William Caslon, established about 1728. There are various minor foundries supplying types at lower rates than the so-called "legitimate"
foundries; but its quality cannot be said to be so good. Exception, however, must be made as regards the Patent Type-
Founding Company, now carried on by Messrs. Shank and
Revell, whose letter is equal to any produced in this country,
and sold at reasonable prices, owing to the possession of the
patent rights of a very beautiful automatic machine invented
by Mr. J. R. Johnson, one of the originators of the concern.

As may be expected in a business conducted on such an
exclusive basis, improvements have been very tardily and somewhat unwillingly introduced. Until a recent period the clumsy
hand mould, known to have been in use two centuries back was
retained. The machine for type-casting was rendered possible
by an expedient invented by an American, Mr. David Bruce,
who, after several Englishmen had failed, succeeded in making
a casting machine, which was brought over here so late as 1848,
previous to which all types were cast by hand.

Several slight improvements have been made in this apparatus, and it is still in use. It was reserved for an entirely non-
practical man, a chemist, to make the first automatic machine.
We refer to Mr. J. R. Johnson's type-caster, patented in 1859
and 1862. It not only casts the type, but rubs and dresses it,
and removes the "break"; in short the type metal is poured
in at one end of the machine and comes out at the other end in
the shape of type fit for immediate use by the printer.

Nor have the English type-founders displayed much inventiveness in designing new faces of types. Most of the fancy
kinds from time to time introduced are brought over from
America and Germany; the English founders merely buying
"strikes" and casting from them. At the present time a
great quantity of foreign type is being used in this country,
especially American, owing to one or two firms having estab-

lished agencies in London. Owing to this fact printers have lately been provided with a variety of founts such as they never had before. The tame, formal, and harsh lines of type, hitherto characteristic of the letter-press method, have been supplemented by combinations in which the most fertile fancy may find expression. The result is seen in the very beautiful specimens of printing that the last twelve months has produced, altogether different in style to anything previously attempted with moveable types.

STEREOTYPING.

THE art of Stereotyping was invented by William Ged, an Edinburgh goldsmith, about 1725. He did some work for the University of Cambridge, but very imperfectly; his progress being impeded, it is said, by the prejudices of the pressmen and compositors. On the death of William Ged, in 1749, his son, James Ged, proposed to carry on the business, but was unable to do so for want of funds, and stereotyping was abandoned for nearly thirty years, when Mr. Alexander Tilloch again invented it, not having heard of Ged's system. He took out a patent in partnership with Foulis, printer to the University of Glasgow, in the year 1784. About 1797, Professor Wilson made some improvements in the system, but up to 1800 the art, although it had been twice invented and practised, had fallen into disuse, and might indeed be said to be almost unknown. Earl Stanhope recognising its utility resorted to Tilloch and Foulis, and obtained practical instructions from them, associating himself also with a London printer named Andrew Wilson. The result was that, in 1802, the plaster process was perfected, and it has since been followed universally, until the introduction of the French or papier mache method.

After the passing of the Reform Bill, in 1832, the newspapers of the country made huge strides in regard to circulation, and the mechanical ingenuity of engineers and others was taxed to the utmost to provide greater facilities for producing a large number of copies in the shortest possible time. In 1846, there was introduced into England by an Italian named Vanoni—by trade a maker of plaster casts of statuary—a system of forming moulds in papier mache. It had been already utilised in France for a short time. Another Italian, James Dellagana, became acquainted with the system in Paris, and came over here to set up a stereotype foundry. He was entrusted with the production of the stereo plates for *The Times*, and soon became the most successful stereotyper of his day. In 1855 he patented an invention for casting solid metal plates type high, and also devised a system for casting these plates hollow inside, but still type high, by the use of a core in the casting box. In 1861 he patented a rolling press for taking the moulds, a great improvement on all previous methods. Between 1856 and 1859 experiments were being made at *The Times* office which led to the most important and permanent results. By 1860 the change from moveable type to stereo plates for newspaper printing had been accomplished. The columns were originally cast type-high and arranged after being planed and finished in a forme of four pages. The next step was to adopt these type columns to the Rotary Applegath presses. Subsequently, instead of separately dealing with columns, the matter was taken from the complete page at one operation. This was done originally with brushes, afterwards with a roller press. In 1863 the culminating point was reached ; plates were cast in a tubular form, cylindrical on the external surface.

In 1864 there was patented a modification of the stereotype process, which, although little noticed at the time, has since given rise to quite a new branch of industry, and has materially enlarged the capabilities of letterpress printing. In that year, Mr. Alfred Leighton took out protection for printing surfaces made of india-rubber, and vulcanized when in the moulds. The business of producing "rubber-stamps" is now very largely carried on in different parts of the country.

Quite recently an innovation has been introduced which may most materially change the future method of the art. It consists in discarding the ordinary metal in which the plates are cast, and using instead, a substance called celluloid. The ingredients of the mould are yellow oxide of lead and glycerine, forming a semi-fluid paste, which is applied to the surface of the type. The matrix is placed with its face upwards on the bed of a powerful press, and on this matrix a heated sheet of celluloid about $\frac{3}{16}$th of an inch is laid, and the platen of the press brought down, which results in a perfect fac-simile being attained upon the celluloid. The plates when taken from under the casting press are ready to be printed from. Whereas a good electrotype from a wood-block generally requires on an average six hours, a cast in celluloid can be got in less than one hour. The celluloid blocks are said to save time in making ready, to be especially easy to handle, and to be very tough. They are not affected by acids, and coloured inks may be used with them. They do not corrode, and are so elastic that they may be bent round small cylinders. Several large printing offices in London and elsewhere have already adopted the celluloid process.

ELECTROTYPING.

CONFLICTING accounts are given of the origin of Electrotyping. The most trustworthy account probably is, that Professor Daniell was the discoverer of the principle on which the deposition of compact copper depends; that Mr. C. J. Jordan was the inventor of the first application of that principle to useful purposes in the art known as electro-metallurgy, and that Mr. Thomas Spencer was one of the improvers. Jordan died, in very straitened circumstances, a compositor, in 1872.

As applied to the production of printing surfaces, however M. Morel, a Frenchman, may be said to be the originator of the art. He was encouraged by Messrs. Cassell & Co. to carry on his experiments, and occupied a stable in the old Belle Sauvage Yard, where the splendid printing establishment of Messrs. Cassell, Petter and Galpin now stands. Morel was the first to adopt wax for taking the moulds, and ultimately perfected the system as now followed. Messrs. Cassell, Petter and Galpin and Messrs. Richardson, Koolman, and Isger are also identified with various substantial improvements in this beautiful art, which has quite recently been accelerated by the adoption of the dynamo-electro machine, instead of the batteries formerly used.

TYPE SETTING.

In the view of a printing office published in 1507, already mentioned, there is a representation of a person setting types, apparently a woman; for even as early as this year in Italy and France there were female compositors. The case includes boxes for both capitals and lower case letters, and all the boxes are of the same size. The copy is held in a cleft stick called the visorum; but in some early offices there is reason to believe a reader, called an anagnoste, was employed, who dictated the matter to the type-setters. The workman holds a composing stick; this latter appliance was not used by our English prototypographer until 1480. Before then, as Mr. Blades has shown, the types were taken straight from their boxes, and placed side by side in a sort of coffin made of hard wood with a stout bottom, and screws at the foot to tighten the page when completed. The width of the page could not be extended beyond the internal measurement of the coffin, but might be reduced at pleasure by placing down either side a piece of wood. The depth would be regulated in a similar manner by varying the thickness of the foot-block against which the screws worked.

The composing sticks (we are still following Mr. Blades) were originally of hard wood, without any sliding adjustment; one set, all the same, were for folio pages, another for quarto, another for octavo.

We need not describe the modern system of composition to practical printers. The inventor of the screw composing stick is not known, nor when iron was substituted for wood. The early books had uneven lines, because placing rough types upon rough types admitted of very little shifting or adjustment, and to this fact the author named attributes the practice of leaving the lines of an uneven length. As already stated, Caxton about 1480 began to make his lines equal by spacing out the words to a certain gauge, and no doubt then adopted the primitive composing stick.

As early as the beginning of the present century, when inventiveness seemed to experience amost remarkable impulse, the irksomeness of setting types in the manner that had been followed for about three centuries began to be complained of, and a machine for composing was discussed. It was not, however, until 1822 that the first English Patent for a Type-setting Machine was taken out by William Church, and during the last sixty years a great number of inventions of the kind have been devised, patented, tested and abandoned. At the present day there are, however, three kinds of machines in actual daily use in this country. One of them was invented by Mr. Robert Hattersley, of Manchester, in 1857, who has since greatly improved it. Another was invented by Mr. Alexander Mackie, of Warrington, in 1865, and this too, has since been modified considerably. The third was invented by Charles Kastenbein, of Brussels, in 1869. Hattersley's machines are used in several newspaper offices in the country. Mackie's (which may be driven by steam) are in operation at a great establishment at Crewe, founded by their inventor. Kastenbein's are adopted not only in some English offices but in many offices abroad.

A very remarkable system of type setting is now in use at *The Times* office. Soon after the Franco-German war the Kastenbein machine was introduced there, but it has ever since been undergoing such modifications in detail as experience from time to time has suggested, until it has now reached a state of great efficiency. The most skilful workman setting up type by hand could not exceed a general average of about 40 lines per hour, or a maximum rate of 50 lines per hour during short periods of great pressure. The machine enables a fair workman to attain an average speed of 100 lines an hour when composing from manuscript, which he has to read for himself. It has been discovered that the speed can be doubled or nearly so when the operator is assisted by a reader, and thus composes from dictation. It has for some time been the custom to transmit the foreign intelligence from Paris, Vienna and Berlin to Printing-house Square by means of Hughes's printing telegraph, and to dictate the contents of the telegraphic slip to a compositor at the machine. By this combination, remarkable facilities in dealing with late manuscript have been obtained, and it has been possible to carry on the work of type setting almost to the time of going to press.

The latest development of this system is one that supersedes the necessity for the transcription of the shorthand notes of the reporters in the Houses of Parliament and their subsequent transmission to the office by messengers. This is effected by the use of the telephone. The wires are laid down in the subway of the Thames Embankment, and a connection formed between the House and the printing office. One of Edison's loud-speaking telephones is placed at either end, and thus the compositor at the composing machine is brought into direct communication with the parliamentary reporter at Westminster. The notes made by the latter are read directly into the telephone-receiver in a room adjoining the gallery, and the compositor at his machine in the office sits with his ears in juxtaposition with the other terminal of the instrument. He is also furnished with a speaking instrument, with a key for ringing a bell and with a bell which is rung from the House. The compositor announces by the bell that he is ready, receives a sentence, strikes the bell to indicate that he understands it, sets up the type with his machine, strikes the bell again for the reader to continue his dictation, and so on until the work is carried as far as time will allow.

PRESSING PRINTED SHEETS.

Until within quite recently, nearly all paper to be printed upon was wetted previous to impression. Lately, however, this has been, to some extent, obviated by the adoption of what is called the " hard packing " system of making ready. Glazed boards and hard paper are used as packing for the machine cylinder instead of an india-rubber or woollen blanket; a most exquisite impression is thus obtained, but a very strong machine and absolute perfection in the manufacture of type render this practicable. Much of the ordinary fine printing is nevertheless done on dry paper which has been previously calendered or rolled.

In the matter of pressing or calendering sheets, to remove the inequalities caused by the pressure, great progress has been made. In the early days of the art printed sheets were folded, gathered

and collated, and then, if to be bound and finished carefully, were
beaten.   The volume being divided into parcels of a few sheets,
these were laid flat on a stone and beaten with a heavy hammer
until the desired smoothness was attained.   The "Hot-press" was
the next means adopted.   Glazed boards were placed alternately
between the sheets, iron plates were heated in the furnace, and one
of each of them was laid between every 20 or 30 sheets until the
press was full, and the whole was pressed down by a lever and
windlass.   This process was, to some extent, superseded by "cold
pressing," glazed boards only being used.   A strong iron screw
standing press was employed, or the greater power of the hydraulic
press.   The latter was, in itself, one of the most useful inventions
of modern times.   It was introduced in 1796 by Joseph Bramah,
of Stainsborough, Yorkshire.   In it water is utilised as an agent
of force—a mechanical power, in fact.   Its disadvantages are
that it is slow in action, complicated in construction, and
irregular in power ; besides being costly and occupying much
room.

Within the last three years, a new kind of standing press
has been brought into notice, known as the "Boomer" press
—an American invention.   The principle of the press is that
that there are four levers or arms connected together, which work
upon toggle joints.   Through these joints passes a screw, cut
right and left-handed.   The rotation of the screw causes the
two joints to approach or recede with an uniform motion.   A
sliding standard runs through the top frame or head-block, and
maintains the accurate horizontal position of the pressing-
plate or follower.   An enormous maximum power at the
moment of reaching the dead centre is obtained by the simplest
mechanical means, and without gearing.

When it became customary to give certain classes of work
a very high glaze, a "rolling machine" was made, wherein the
sheets were placed between plates of copper or zinc, and passed
in rapid succession between two hard or chilled steel cylinders.
This was a tedious process, and the plates had to be frequently
cleaned, lest the set-off of the ink should soil the sheets.

The most important alteration of this system has, however,
been effected by the introduction of Gill's hot rolling machine,

manufactured by Furnivall & Co., of Manchester. It dries, presses, and calenders sheets direct from the printing machine, doing away with the necessity for drying rooms, press boards, and hydraulic presses. It works as fast as sheets can be fed in, presses perfectly, and leaves no set-off. The machine may or may not be adapted to compress the paper. When it is desirable that a book should be made as thin as possible, a very remarkable effect is produced, as in the case of the "London Post-Office Directory," which, immediately after the machine was used, was reduced $1\frac{1}{2}$ inches in thickness without making the print less legible. The set-off is wiped from the rolls as they revolve by a series of sponge bags in troughs containing a solution of common soda and water.

A dry pressing machine, invented by Mr. J. W. Jones, State Superintendent of Printing, Harrisburg, Pennsylvania, has been introduced into this country during the past twelve months, which is said to do more work than the Gill machine, but not quite so well, and at small expense.

ENGRAVING ON METAL.

THIS most important invention is claimed for Tommaso Finiguerra, a Florentine goldsmith, who, in 1452, in the course of his niello work, by chance laid the plate, when it had been filled with blackened oil, on a piece of damp linen, and thus got an impression. The hint thus given was quickly improved upon by the artists of that age, and engraving upon metal plates began to take rank as a fine art. Finiguerra may be said to be the first to do for art what Gutenberg did for literature.

A good engraving is a marvel of beautiful mechanism. It requires an amount of painstaking, skill, and labour that seems almost incredible. Many important plates have occupied their engraver from three to six years. The engraving issued by the Art Union of London in 1875, the subject of which was Maclise's fresco, the meeting of Blucher and Wellington, after the battle of Waterloo, entailed upon the engraver, Mr. Lumb Stocks, R.A., no less than five years' work, for which he was paid the sum of £3,500. Line engraving has for some years been steadily declining. When a painting can be photographed in three minutes, or copied in chromo-lithography at a very small expense, engravers cannot afford, unless supported by such institutions as the Art Union of London, to spend years in study and preparation, and three years working upon a single plate. Owing to such causes some of the best painters and engravers have abandoned it.

The following is an outline of the different processes of plate engraving.

Line engraving is the highest style of the art. The design is made by incisions on a copper or steel plate, cut by the graver or burin, and the various effects of light and shade, distance and perspective, the textures of accessories and drapery, flesh tints and the expression of features, are all produced by a corresponding variety of lines engraved into the plate.

To take an impression from this plate, its surface is covered with a thick oily ink, so that all the lines are effectually filled. As this smears the entire plate, the printer next rubs off the superfluous ink, first with a cloth, and then with the palms of his hands. The surface is now clean, but the ink still remains in all the lines or incisions. The sheet of paper which is to receive the impression is then damped and laid upon a plate, and both are passed under the roller of the press, covered with a blanket, the elasticity of which forces the moist paper to enter the indentations of the plate, the result being that the ink is transferred from the incisions in the plate to the sheet of paper.

Next in importance to line engraving comes *Etching ;* indeed some authorites give this process the first place. In etching the plate is first covered with a coat of wax or rosin, which is dissolved by heat and allowed to harden. The tool used is the point, or etching needle. With this the lines and dots of the design are traced through the wax on to the surface of the copper plate. Aquafortis is then poured on, and this powerful acid eats into the copper wherever a line has been made, the wax meanwhile protecting the other parts. After repeated bitings by aquafortis according to the effect desired, the plate is cleaned from the acid and wax, and is then ready to be printed from in the same manner as a line engraving.

The characteristics of line engraving are beautiful precision and symmetry of form, while the etching excels in freedom and sketchiness. Long years of practice are essential to the former ; the latter can be produced after a little technical study by any one who can draw. Hence when a painter undertakes to engrave one of his own designs he naturally resorts to etching ; on the other hand, when a professional engraver undertakes to make an elaborate reproduction of an important painting, line engraving is employed.

Etching has taken a new development in England now that Professor Legros has started etching classes both at the Slade School and at South Kensington. Owing to these influences it threatens, except for very large and important plates, to oust even mezzotint as the means of translation into black and white. Its most recent venture has been the direct transfer of likeness to the etching plate.

The *mezzotint* process, called also the *manière noire* or *Anglaise* by French writers, was carried to great perfection about a century ago in England. The plate is first roughened uniformly all over, so that if it were then inked and printed from, it would print a solid black. The rough surface is then scraped away according to the effect required, those parts most smoothed taking the least ink, and so producing the highest lights, while the parts least scraped away produce the deepest shadows. After long neglect mezzotint has recently been revived by English engravers, and is attracting much admiration, particularly in landscape.

In *stipple* engraving the effect is produced entirely by dots or holes punched into the plate. This process has been much used for the flesh parts in portraits, but very few of the prints in stipple work have a reputation in art, except perhaps the graceful vignettes engraved by Bartolozzi towards the end of the last century.

Bank Note engraving has been brought to high perfection, especially in America. The plates and dies are engraved on steel in the line manner ; in addition to this, beautiful mechanical effects are produced by the complicated geometrical lathe. Except with regard to bank note work a " steel engraving " is only a figure of speech; what are so called are only engraved on copper, which is a much mellower material to work on than steel. All the great prints of former ages were done on copper-plates and not on steel, as is commonly supposed.

The capabilities of copper-plate printing have been very greatly increased by the discovery of a process for steel-facing the plates. They are laid, after being cleaned, in a trough containing the solution, and allowed to remain for a certain time, when they are coated with a film of steel. They may then be printed from in the usual way. Previous to this discovery, plates, after a few impressions, became worn away in the finer parts, and had to be constantly retouched if a large number of impressions was required. Even the later proofs were very inferior to the early ones. By using the steel-facing process, the plate itself need never become worn—as soon as one coating becomes worn another can be applied. In this way, the Art Union, already mentioned, supplies its subscribers with thousands of copies of its engravings, the last impression being in every respect equal to the first. This process was patented some years ago by Messrs. Bradbury, Wilkinson & Co., of Farringdon Road, who practise it on a large scale.

The copper-plate press has undergone but little alteration from its earliest known form to that in use at the present day. It consists of two upright checks, with ribs at right angles to them. A short distance above these ribs is a solid iron cylinder, made to revolve by a star handle, connected with the axis, the radii of this star being as long as the height from the ground will permit. A carriage containing the plate is made to run along the ribs. Beneath the ribs is another cylinder, which is made to rise by means of a lever, and press the carriage against the upper cylinder as it passes along the press with any required force. It is a dreadfully slow process; and to give an idea of the tediousness of copper-plate printing, it may be mentioned that it took altogether fifty minntes to produce each impression of the plate referred to.

Many attempts have been made, however, to expedite the system of copper-plate printing, and almost entirely without success, by the invention of a machine more or less automatic which should supersede the method of cleaning, inking, and pressing the plate. The first really practicable machine of the kind was shown at the Paris Exposition Universelle of 1878. It was originally invented by Mons. C. Guy, a Frenchman, in 1876. There were two machines shown, each of them it was claimed would produce from 6,000 to 9,000 copies per day. After the plate was inked it was subjected to the action of a series of pads, while a number of bands revolving rapidly polished the plate—which was placed on a block like an electro-type—and removed the superfluous ink. The warming was effected by a moving tube underneath the table. The impression was given by a cylinder as in a lithographic machine. M. Guy devised another machine for printing by the copper-plate method from plates curved round a cylinder, but it was not shown. Both machines have been tried and found successful at Messrs. Bradbury, Wilkinson & Co.'s. One of them will be shown in the present Exhibition.

ENGRAVING ON WOOD.

A wood engraving of St. Christopher, now in the collection of Earl Spencer, was long supposed to be the most ancient example of engraving, as a fine art, but prints have lately been discovered bearing dates as early as 1418 and 1406.

During the last thirty years the art of Wood Engraving has entered into a new phase—indeed, excepting what was done with Doré's earlier drawings, it has made the departure within the last ten years. Previously it was thought that beyond certain formal limits the engraver should not enter. A certain kind of line, it was held, should be used to represent ground; another kind to represent foliage, another to represent sky, another flesh, another drapery, and so on. Each sort of line was the orthodox symbol for a certain form, and if by chance or inexperience it was not used by the artist in his original drawing the omission was expected to be supplied by the engraver. Of late, however, the publishers of illustrated periodicals have increased the range of their illustrations. The perpetual recurrence of old conventional lines became tiresome. Photography was used for transferring paintings or drawings on canvas or paper direct to the wood. The art of wood engraving received in consequence a fresh impulse, and entered into a new liberty, the possibilities of which it is yet too soon to estimate. Instead of merely symbolising the work of the artist, the engraver now makes use of all methods by which he can fix on the block as accurately and perfectly as possible the original picture that has been put into his hand for reproduction. The abandonment of the conventional recipes is the distinguishing characteristic of the new school. Its finest triumphs are not three years old and may be said to have begun with exact reproductions of the effect of drawing on rough paper with a large black lead. The next step was the exact reproduction of water colour body, black and white chiefly. Then came the reproduction of water colour washes, crayon and charcoal, and last of all, brush marks in oil. The *ultima thule* is regarded as the successful reproduction of brush marks with the graver. It is now held that the beauty of a wood engraving does not consist in the beauty of its lines, for when held from the eye at a distance of three times its diagonal the lines are not seen at all, and that when the engraving so closely resembles an original drawing that no difference can be detected between the two, the highest possibilities of the art have been achieved. The old school of engravers, of course, strongly oppose these modern heresies.

PROCESS BLOCKS.

This term is employed in printing offices to describe printing surfaces for the letter-press process obtained by other means than engraving. In the " Gillotype " process, invented by M. Gillot, of Paris, a plate of zinc was drawn upon with a suitable ink, and rosin was powdered over it. The rosin adhered only to those places to which ink had been applied, and was easily removed from the other parts. Afterwards, for the purpose of obtaining a relief block, the plate was placed on the bottom of a shallow trough containing very dilute sulphuric or hydrochloric

acid. By means of a rocking motion given to the box the acid
was caused to pass slowly and continually to and fro over
the surface of the plate. When the etching mixture was removed
after a certain interval a relief block was obtained, in which it
was only necessary to remove the large whites.

This invention formed the foundation upon which subsequent
ones with a similar object rest. Alterations have been made
in details, but the various systems of "typographic etching,"
"automatic engraving," and processes known under the names
of different practitioners, are merely developments. The art has
been carried to great perfection, and some "blocks" so produced
are only distinguishable from casts of wood engravings by
experts. Many of the pictorial journals are thus "illustrated,"
the blocks costing only a fraction of the price of those engraved
in the ordinary way.

GLYCERINE TABLETS.

WITHIN the last twelve or eighteen months a new kind of printing, by transfer from glycerine tablets has been invented, and
has already been so extensively practised as to render it quite
a commonplace and ordinary thing. It is somewhat akin to
lithography. The original inventor took a slab composed of
glycerine and some other ingredients, and wrote on a hard glazed
paper with an aniline ink. The writing-ink when pressed down
upon the tablet was absorbed by the latter, and when a clean
sheet of paper was applied and rubbed down upon it with the
fingers, the ink was reproduced upon the paper, giving an exact
copy. In this way fifty or more fac-similes can be made of a
writing or drawing. Under the name of "chromographs,"
"hektographs," and other modern Greek coinages ending with the
word "graph," thousands of these tablets have been sold for use
by the public, and for some purposes the system has become a
formidable rival to lithography. Some years ago a system of
reproducing writings and drawings, invented by M. Zuccato,
and called the "Papyrograph," was introduced, and was largely
patronised. In this a kind of stencil was used, made of paper,
etched, so to speak, by the writing ink employed.

LITHOGRAPHY.

THIS is the only process of printing concerning which we have
an authentic account of its origin. It was invented by Aloys
Senefelder, born at Prague in 1771. He lost his father—a
musician at one of the Munich theatres—when young, and was
thrown on his resources to obtain a livelihood. He tried to
support himself as a professor of music, and not being able to
pay for the engraving of his compositions, he resolved to engrave
them himself. He found this both expensive and difficult, and
then tried to work with a greasy ink on copper, to etch this
afterwards in relief, and to print the plate with the ordinary
type printing press. One day, having occasion to write down a
memorandum, and having no paper at hand, he wrote it with
his composition ink on a polished piece of Kelheim or Solenh ofen
stone. It occurred to him afterwards to raise this writing with acid
and print with a press of his own invention. From this beginning
he gradually discovered the whole process of chemical printing
from stone. His first work—a piece of music—was printed by lithography in 1796, and in 1800 he patented his invention in Bavaria
and most of the German states. A detailed account of the origin of
the art will be found in Senefelder's own book, "Vollständiges
Lehrbuch der Steindruckerey," (Munich, 1818, 4to.) an English
translation of which was issued by R. Ackermann.

We are not in possession of such a trustworthy history of the
progress of the art and its diffusion abroad. It is known, however, that the city where the art was discovered, was the place
where it was originally practised with the greatest success.
Soon after 1800, Manlich and Aretin set up litho' presses and
published a collection of drawings of ancient masters belonging
to the king of Bavaria. In 1801, the art was spread all over
Germany; in 1802, Senefelder set up an office in Vienna. In 1807,
André, of Offenbach, a partner of Senefelder, tried unsuccessfully
to start a lithographic office in London and Paris. In 1810,
the French government refused permission to Manlich to introduce the business in Paris, on the ground, it is believed, that it
furnished too many facilities for forgery. The pioneer of lithography in France was Godefroy Engelmann, who established
himself in Paris in 1816. The art was introduced into England

by Charles Hullmandel, who was a friend of Senefelder, and came to London, where he set up a press at his lodgings in Great Marlborough Street in 1820. Mr. Rudolph Ackermann, the picture publisher, warmly encouraged the new process, and induced many artists of eminence to cultivate it. In 1826, another London office was started by Engelmann, Graf, and Coindet. Soon after this Mr. Michael Hanhart founded an establishment, which has up to the present day enjoyed great eminence.

Chromo-lithography was projected by Senefelder, but practically realised by Godefroy Engelmann in 1836.

The original press of Senefelder was a very different apparatus from the present hand press, as may be seen from the drawing attached to his English specification.

In regard to the Lithographic Machine, it may be stated that its introduction has increased the speed at which lithographic impressions can be obtained nearly twenty-fold; that is, nearly seven hundred copies per hour, instead of only three hundred or four hundred per day. The first successful lithographic machine was the invention of a German, named Siegel. It had a scraper, which, when the sheet was brought over the stone, was lowered so as to press on the leather of a travelling tympan, and thus the impression was produced. The stones were damped by a kind of water trough or ductor. About 1860 the cylindrical printing machine was introduced from France. It had no damping apparatus, it being requisite during the working of them to moisten the stone by hand. Later, Messrs. Robinson, of Bristol, produced a litho' machine of somewhat different construction, although the inking was the same and the damping done by hand. There was, however, no means of securing register. In 1863 Mr. William Conisbee patented a lithographic machine, but it was not perfected for some time afterwards. The stone was damped without having recourse to manual labour. Accuracy of register was secured by means of a pointing apparatus in connection with the feeding board. The box or coffin in which the stone was set was so arranged that the old method of packing or bringing up the surface by means of pieces of millboard was done away with; and other great improvements were effected. In short, Mr. Conisbee may be said to be the practical inventor of the modern lithographic machine.

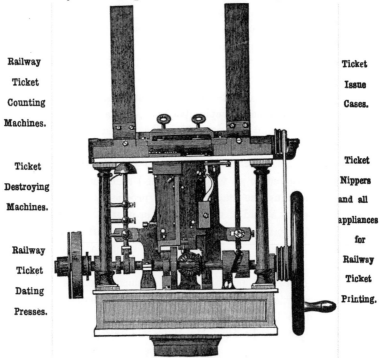

PAPER AND STATIONERY.

BY

W. F. CATCHESIDE.

No. 1.—PAPER.

PAPER, what is it ? Some of our dictionaries give the following definition—" A thin flexible substance used for writing and printing on." This is not a correct answer to the query ; it does not embody the exact character of paper except in the one word " flexible." It is difficult to say what paper is. The most correct answer in these days would be " the product of a paper-mill," seeing that so many varieties of paper are made.

With the exception of iron and wood, perhaps paper occupies the most important place in the list of materials which provide the most useful appliances in civilized life. What would the world in its present state do without paper ? It is the object of this essay, to show what multitudinous uses the article known as " paper " fulfils, and the numerous forms of this substance as manufactured by papermakers.

The early history of paper is not very clearly defined. A common belief credits the Egyptians with the foremost position among ancient papermakers. Other authorities praise the Chinese for first discovering the art of papermaking. It is not the purpose of the writer to enter into any discussion, much more attempt any solution of this question. Suffice it to say that the preparation of a substance upon which graphic characters could be delineated and preserved is of very ancient date. We have record of the " tables of stone " upon which the ten commandments were inscribed, and it is quite feasible to suppose that a substitute for stone was made the object of inquiry by the learned men of ancient times. The main features of the substitute would be, an even surface, strength, and an ability to stand the test of preservation.

In looking to Nature, who provided the stone, plants in due course were examined. It is curious to note that wood was not extensively used, owing, probably to its facility of decay. In the present day, wood can be divested of its elements of decay by chemical processes; unknown of course to the ancients. Though many hard woods are to be found in the East, the seekers after fibre, or the writing substance, seem to have been aware of the unstable nature of all woody fibrous bodies. It is worthy of note, that to-day, plants and, practically speaking, the same supplies of Nature, furnish the modern papermaker with his raw material.

Ancient papermaking had apparently the same objects in view as we pursue in the present day. We treat material or raw fibres to-day, it is true, with more perfect means and more perfect result ; but with the same object. We produce from the raw materials a substance that will permit of graphic delineation ; that is of a lighter colour than the graphic fluid ; that is flexible ; that is capable of being easily and generally used ; free from the physical difficulty of being cumbersome, and finally, a substance that is capable of preservation in all ages.

The ancients used such materials as their knowledge of the world suggested. The Egyptians found in the *papyrus*, a reed which grew abundantly on the banks of the Nile, a raw material which provided a fibre, sufficiently capable of purification for their purposes. Their processes of purifying the *papyrus* were naturally crude, and were directed probably to the removal of certain constituents which provoked fermentation and decay in the natural fibre. In eliminating these, Egyptian papermakers reckoned to obtain a white fibre and a substance which would keep intact, and thereby preserve inscribed characters in a convenient, yet perfect form.

In regard to papyrus, Pliny, and other Roman authors, give very circumstantial accounts of the finding upon the Janiculum of the books of Numa, written upon papyrus. Pliny states also the means that had been used for their preservation. This would carry their date back to the seventh century B.C. ; but the history of Rome at that time is known to be doubtful. It is quite certain, however, that these books were destroyed because they contained expositions of philosophy, possibly of religious belief, certainly of ritual observances at variance with those held at the time when they were found. This would indicate their origin from an earlier people. It is known that on the site of Rome there was a city before its Roman occupation. There is still better evidence in the papyrus rolls found in Egyptian mummies. Some of the writing on the latter has been deciphered, and is believed to be of the time of the Pharoahs.

The account of the mode of manufacture is mainly derived from Pliny. He describes the stalk as triangular and being cut into slices, which were split into very thin leaves by a needle, taking care to have them as broad as possible : the best taken from the inside. These were laid upon an inclined table, side by side, as long as the slices from the papyrus would allow. They were then trimmed to equal length, being moistened with the Nile water, which in a muddy state, was said to have the properties of glue. Upon these a similar row of strips was placed at right angles, and the whole pressed—according to other accounts, beaten together.

This account is evidently imperfect ; in fact, no representation of their processes from such nations as the Egyptians, the Japanese or the Chinese, are entirely reliable. This is due partly to the misinterpretation of foreign narrators and partly from the undoubted suppression of some of the particulars by the natives. But by the aid of modern science fair discrimination between what is true and what is false is possible.

The gluey properties of the muddy Nile waters do not exist. Pliny, however, mentions other forms of papyrus, in which he describes a flour paste as being used, and, moreover, he gives directions for its preparation. There is also incidental mention made of the mallet by which it was beaten, showing that possibly the cross layers were indeed incorporated by that instrument.

This is in substance all that was known of the formation of papyrus. The solution of the problem depends upon microscopic examination. For papyrus this was first done by Dr. Wiesner. He showed that the papyrus plant, *Cyperus papyrus*, like all solid endogens, has a solid pith, with continuous longitudinal cell formation, and, more than this, with continuous air

spaces in the pith cells as in all water plants.   Here we can
understand that the continuous cells give the strength in the two
directions as they are crossed.

Dr. Julius Wiesner, in his work, "Einleitung in die
Technische Mikroscopie" (1837), gives an interesting account
of a microscopic examination of papyrus paper.   Dr. Wiesner
found that, in all the specimens examined by him, there were
not two, but three layers, at once differing from the ancient
accounts.   A closer examination will explain more.   A needle,
not a knife, was used to cut the layers.   The former would pass
between the cells, while the latter might cut them ; still more
the pith cells round the air spaces would be severed, leaving
their fibres free, and in the process of beating these would be
more or less interknit.

Papyrus, then, is a pith paper, accompanied with the strength
of two or three plaitings of cell fibre, which alone could give the
paper real tenacity.

At best, papyrus had no great strength, consisting as it did
so much of pith cells.   We learn from the ancients that only
the best kinds were made, without the writing running through
to the reverse side ; and we have the testimony of existing
manuscripts to show that, after every five or six leaves, a sheet
of parchment was interposed, to give strength to the rolls.

Papyrus continued to be used even into comparatively
modern times ; and after true modern paper had been manufactured, certain official documents, papal bulls, &c., were
continued to be issue upon it.

Having given a short account of this ancient process of
papermaking, we can compare for a moment, in our mind's eye,
as it were, these old processes with the routine of a first class
paper mill in the present day; and there are many curious
thoughts to be gained from such a *reverie*.   If we place together
a sheet of ancient paper and a sheet of superfine writing, what
wonderful stages must have existed between the production of
the two !   If we think of papermaking as an art illustrated by the
two specimens, we must pride ourselves upon the progress and
improvement that papermaking has undergone.   A shrivelled,
yellow-looking, coarse sheet of fibre has but few attractions, whilst
a sheet of fine paper is " a joy for ever."

Further, this great gulf represents great personal study and inventive power, continuous application and perseverance. Papermakers throughout all ages seem to have been very busy, and determined to perfect their art; yet, when the ages that have elapsed since the Egyptian papyrus sheets were made, are taken into consideration, the manufacture of paper has been invested with a spirit of conservatism, a spirit which even to this hour wraps the paper mill as with a dark mantle. Improvements are made, but slowly made.

As before mentioned, it is not possible within the scope of an essay such as the present to devote much space to any historical details of papermaking. The present is a prosaic age, and the attractions of the hour, as a rule, overwhelm the fascinations of antiquity. Therefore, let us take a leap from the old ages to modern times, and plunge into the paper trade of 1880.

Modern papermakers would divide paper into two great classes, viz.: 1st, paper that is to receive graphic characters; and 2nd, paper for other purposes than this. A closer view of paper would reveal a subdivision as follows :—

1st Class of Paper—
    a. Writing Paper.
    b. Drawing Paper.
    c. Printing Paper.
2nd Class of Paper—
    a. Wrapping Paper.
    b. Special and uncommon Papers.

The first class of paper comprises, under the headings *a, b* and *c*, a great number of papers which will be enumerated by-and-bye, whilst the varieties embodied in the second class will also receive due mention. Previous to doing this, a short outline of papermaking, with explanations of certain terms as applied to paper, may be found interesting.

All kinds of paper have, to a certain stage in the operations of manufacture, one common process. The raw material has to undergo certain operations, necessary individually to all classes of paper. Paper is made from a substance containing fibre. The substance is valuable as a raw material in just proportion to the quantity and quality of fibre it contains, and the means that must be employed to obtain the fibre. Though far behind, from a scientific point of view, the crude methods of the ancients are still the test of a good fibre so far as the facility of obtaining the fibre is concerned.

However fine a fibre may be, if it can only be obtained at a great expense, it is worse than useless. The next point is to be certain of a plentiful supply of the fibre. Small specimens are of no practical use, and no fibre that cannot, in these days, be obtained in quantity is of any value to the papermaker. The supply must, moreover, be regular in both quantity and quality. It is a noteworthy fact that new fibres are, after their introduction and adoption, speedily sorted into certain marks, denoting certain qualities. These assortments are most essential, and are the very life and soul of a fibre merchant's business. Their regularity of quality is the papermaker's security against fluctuation in his classes of paper, and too much importance cannot be laid upon this point. Impurities, not to use the ugly word adulteration, should also be strictly looked after, and there are several substances that receive special attention in examining fibre supplies. These remarks apply to all fibres.

The best papers are now produced from rags. The rags come from the waste of factories and mills, these varieties being known as "new cuttings," and are the most expensive; from collectors in large cities and from government stores, institutions and other large communities producing rags of all kinds. The small collectors or rag-shop keepers buy their stock from the "pickers." These people, generally of the poorest class, scavenge the streets for all waste material—such as bones, rags, iron, paper, cloth, metal, &c., and convey all their heterogenous collection to the rag shop, where a hasty glance from the buyer assesses their value in bulk for ready cash. The shopkeeper sorts the collection, the rags being kept separate. In some instances the rags are submitted to further separation, and certain qualities of higher value are put aside. The small shopkeeper, in his turn, takes his rags to the dealer, who buys them in bulk, mixed miscellaneously, for cash also. Often the rags, paper, old rope, matting, and all other fibrous substance are mixed together, and prove a good test for the dealer's knowledge of his trade. A comprehensive price is offered to the dealer, who then sorts the parcel carefully. Linen. and cotton rags are separated—clean and dirty, whole and torn, large and small are divided, and each classified according to a standard of comparison fixed by the dealer.

Further sub-division takes place. The linens and cottons are classed according to quality. Hence, " fines " are better than "outshots," and thirds are inferior still. All waste substances are dealt with in the same way. Each variety is diligently examined and divided into qualities according to age, strength, cleanliness, size and colour. The following Table will throw a little light upon this subject :—

TABLE I.

WASTE SUBSTANCES.

RAGS.		
New Cuttings	...	Either linen or cotton—the trimmings from large pieces, the cuttings from hosiers, and makers of linen and cotton garments, &c.
Fine Linens ...	...	Best, largest, and cleanest pieces of white linen rags, such as table linen, under-linen, &c., &c.
Fine Cottons...	...	Same, but of cotton goods.
S.P.F.F.F. ...	...	First quality of white German linens.
S.P.F.F. ...	...	Second do. do. do.
S.P.F.	...	Third do. do. do.
F.F.	...	Half-bleached German linens.
L.F.B.	...	Fine blue linens (foreign).
L.F.X.	...	Grey do. do.
Fines	...	Best selected white rags.
Seconds... ...	...	A second quality of do.
Outshots ...	...	White rags rejected from fines.
Thirds	...	Third and lowest quality of white rags.
Common Bagging...		Sacking and used corn, potato, fruit, or meal bagging.
Best Gunny ...	...	The outer wrappers of cotton bales, tea chests, and other similar articles.

OTHER WASTES.

Ropes ... ... The rigging and old ropes of ships.

String ... ... The parcel string waste from the G.P.O. and other sources.

Jute, Flax & Cotton The mill wastes from the spinning and manufacture of cotton and hemp cloths.

Wastepapers... ... The cuttings, shavings, trimmings, &c., of books, pamphlets, and note papers; old account books, letters, S.O. papers, telegrams, &c.; books, newspapers, and brown papers.

France and Russia afford large supplies of rags to our papermakers, and their goods are known in our markets under different brands, which represent a division or classification of quality similar to the above. There is no necessity, and certainly no space at disposal, to give a detailed list of all the various brands representing the rags and wastes of continental or home dealers. The above list may be taken merely as a sign of the existence of the brands.

There is, however, another class of fibres, distinct from what may be called "wastes." Nature provides certain fibres which have proved of immense benefit to papermakers. Prominent among these are: wood, straws, and esparto grass. Many others have been introduced to the trade, but none have proved of any practical value.

Unquestionably the cereal straws have provided the great supply of natural fibre, hitherto. Esparto was introduced to the trade some years ago, and has proved a useful fibre, of good strength, texture and cleanly qualities. Of still later years, wood-pulp has made great strides, and is, some people say, the " fibre of the future."

The preparation of straw for the papermaker is not a very arduous operation. The first essential is cleanliness and freedom from weeds. When this is assured, and, if necessary, actually secured by hand examination, the straw, oat preferably, is cut into chaff, and is then ready for treatment.

Esparto is a species of strong grass, and grows in Africa and Spain. It is impossible to devote any space to its cultivation, varieties, or other characteristics in a short essay like the present; it may therefore be said that the Spanish variety is the best, and that from Algiers the second in quality.

Wood-pulp is prepared in two ways, first, by chemically treating the wood from the pine and aspen trees, and, second, by reducing the same materials to pulp by mechanical means. In the first case, the wood is "shaved" into small pieces and boiled in alkali at 150lbs. pressure; in the second place, the wood is ground by stones under water, to a powder, which floats away, and is collected and pressed into pulp, semi-wet or dry. This last process is chiefly carried on in Norway and Sweden, where the raw material is abundant.

Having thus hastily enumerated the raw material, we will follow its manipulation into paper. The rags, sorted again at the paper mill for safety, are cut, dusted, weighed, and put into a boiler, which may either revolve or be stationary. In general, the boiler revolves, and is always heated by steam being passed into the boiler. The lid is secured, though no great amount of pressure is needed. The boiler generally contains about one ton or so of rags, and is filled with an alkaline lye, made from soda ash, lime, or a mixture of both. The alkali has the effect of cleansing the rag from grease of all kinds and making it perfectly clean. The rags are boiled for a certain number of hours, when the steam is turned off, and the lid of the boiler removed. The boiler revolves half round, so that the rags fall out into a suitable receptacle below, in which they are washed with both hot and cold water. The dirty water runs away continuously, as the bottom of the receptacle or washing tank is perforated with holes, of such size as will not, however, allow the fibre to escape. As soon as the rags are thoroughly cleansed from alkali, they are put into a bleaching chest, also fitted with perforated tiles. Here they are mixed with a solution of chloride of lime, which deprives them of their colouring matter, and in course of a few hours turns them a pure white colour.

This process is now generally conducted in a different manner, though for the same purpose. The rags from the boiler are bleached in the "engine," a circular iron vessel fitted with a powerful wheel, which, revolving at high speed, causes the rags to move round and round the vessel, thereby continually exposing them to the air and light. This is in every way superior to the old system of chest bleaching. The engine is fitted with an ingenious " washer." This is merely a wire gauze drum which dips a few inches below the surface of the liquid in the engine. As the pulp goes round, the drum revolves and the liquid, penetrating the wire gauze, and being carried upwards by the circular shape and motion of the drum, can thus be removed automatically, as it were. As soon as the bleaching has been effected, the drum is set revolving and the liquor becomes exhausted. Fresh water is, however, being continually supplied, so that in time the drum carries away the liquor until the washings through the wire gauze become as pure as the water which enters the engine.

In either case the result sought and obtained is the same, viz., the bleaching of the fibre. Having been bleached, the rags are next " beaten " in the beater, a vessel in all respects similar to the " engine " mentioned above. In the beating engine, the bleached pulp is beaten by the revolving wheel into a very fine state, resembling gruel. This fine pulp can now be called paper in a liquid state. It is at this stage that colours are added, if tinted papers are required. The colour, be it smaltz, ultramarine, or any aniline colour, is simply put into the engine, and the circulation therein soon causes the whole pulp to be equally imbued with the colouring matter.

The process of preparing the fibre ends, it may be said, at this point. The treatment of rags applies generally to all the " wastes." In some instances, such as with old ropes and sacking, the pulp, is not bleached to a white colour, nor is it obtained in as fine a state previous to being made into the coarse qualities of paper.

The natural fibres are treated in much the same way, generally. They are boiled in a boiler with alkaline lye; bleached and beaten as the rags are. But there are many differences of treatment which arise from the physical and chemical differences between rags and the natural fibres. Taking straw and esparto to represent the natural fibres, the first essential difference of treatment is in the boiling. Not only

are these fibres hard and harsh, but they contain silica, fatty
and greasy substances, which require a very strong alkaline liquor
to extract. The extra strength of liquor is further supplemented
by certain grades of pressure in the boiler varying from 40 lbs.
to 115 lbs. according to circumstances. When time is a serious
matter, strong liquors and strong pressures are used in boiling;
otherwise, moderate liquors and moderate pressures are sufficient.

The subject of boiling fibres, it will be apparent to the
outside public, is of immense importance to the papermakers.
Here is, at any rate, one grave source of loss or profit. Loss
to the careless, profit to the skilful. In boiling a ton or two tons
of fibre in the same vessel, in the same liquor, and under every
other similar surrounding, it is easy to see how necessary is
regularity of fibre. Hard lumps, knots, thick pieces, or any
other singular eccentricities among the general mass in the
boiler will damage the result by preventing that even quality
which should always characterise a "boil," as a boiler full of
pulp is termed in the mill.

Great care is therefore necessary to avoid such fibres as
expose the papermaker to this danger. In straw, the knots are
an inevitable trouble and source of specks and spots in paper,
hence it can never be used for good papers. Another point has
to be taken note of; the same liquor which will effectually
cleanse a soft fibre will not have sufficient power to boil a hard
substance. Hence different fibres require suitable boiling liquors.
The strength of the alkaline lye has to be made a special study,
and it is only by trial and actual experiment that a certain
margin can be laid down. Economy in alkali is vital to the
success of a paper mill, whilst any boil, insufficiently treated
through parsimonious allowance, is just as fatal. The outer world
can now appreciate the skill and tact required to prepare the
material for the newspaper that lays upon the breakfast table.

There are many papermakers who do not approve of high
pressure boiling, or of revolving boilers, whilst open and
stationary boilers have equally numerous and strenuous enemies.
It is here only possible to allude briefly to this subject. High
pressure boiling saves time, and when time is more valuable
than a good result, this system pays. It is impossible to expect

that spasmodic violent action will produce strength in the substance acted upon. Just as a fibre will sustain a gradually enforced strain with more certainty than a sudden jerk, so will a fibre issue from a long-continued course of gentle treatment as pure as from a violent action, but unmaimed and unshattered in physical condition. The rotary motion aids circulation in the boiler, and can scarcely have any serious effect upon the fibre. Apart from the dangers attending high pressure boiling, and the extra expense of the plant and machinery, the system is bad, because it is an extreme.

The washing of the boiled fibres is conducted in much the same way as before, viz., in tanks, moveable or stationary, fitted with perforated bottoms. But in washing fibres that have been boiled with strong alkaline lyes, there is every effort made to preserve the strong liquor and recover from it the alkali used in the first instance. For this purpose the liquor is saved by suitable appliances, and evaporated to dryness in large ovens, where it is subsequently fired, and burnt or furnaced. The ash contains the soda, the alkali always used, as carbonate of soda chiefly, and by boiling this with lime a decomposition takes place, and the caustic soda in a clear state, pure enough for use, is obtained. In doing this—an operation that looks easy upon paper—many difficulties occur. Firstly, the liquor requires a large quantity of coal ; the liquor frequently solidifies and is burnt, and the evaporating-pan thereby seriously injured, whilst the furnaces are, ever and anon, wanting repairs. Add to this the cost of lime, steam, and labour employed in re-causticising, and heavy items appear against the value of the recovered soda ash. Without discussing its claims in any way, this process is carried on in a great many paper mills, and is a source of profit and a great convenience. In these days, when the pollution of a river consists in disturbing piscatorial arrangements, our papermakers have had to contend with the great difficulty of satisfying the sages, whose function it is to interfere with all industries that appear in any way indifferent to the sanctity of fish. Notwithstanding the self-evident fact of rivers being the natural drains of the country, and springs and the feeders of rivers being the natural water supply of man, legislation has done its best to fetter the papermaker, to whom the fish looks for his daintiest fare.

Leaving the subject of river pollution and the boiling and and washing of fibre, the next step is to bleach the pulp. This is done exactly as in rags, but with more chloride of lime and less care. There is much room for economy and its *contra* here. The deep tanks used by some papermakers are a great mistake. The action of light is very essential to the bleaching process, and unless the deep tanks are constantly being agitated, there is loss of result. It would pay to have these removed at once. Not to wait until they are worn out, or to resign ourselves to the conclusion that they must do yet awhile. Unfortunately there is very much of this lassitude and want of energy in the paper trade, a trade that is almost dependent in these days of competition on the ready adoption of new improvements.

Bleaching in the engine is a great improvement, and saves both time and trouble, besides having the advantages of a more perfect process of manipulation. In using natural fibres, it is found necessary to wash the bleached pulp in drainers, and not completely in the engine. This is for economy of time only, as the necessity of having a good supply of bleached pulp on hand ready for the beater would occupy too many bleaching engines. The pulp is therefore run into drainers; where it may be washed with additional water to complete the drum washing, and there the bleached stock can lay awaiting the beating engine. It is very desirous to thoroughly cleanse the pulp from every residue of chloride of lime. A general and ready test in the mill is to taste some of the pulp; if any chlorine be present, the senses will soon detect its unpleasant existence. A better test is to squeeze some pulp, and mix with the water therefrom some extract of logwood, or any similar unstable colour. Any free chlorine in the washings will soon discolor the tint of the solution.

Bleaching powder has a deleterious effect upon fibres, rendering them brittle and giving them a greasy character, thereby greatly impeding the washing process. Whilst an excess of bleaching powder will undoubtedly give a bright colour to the pulp, it causes weakness and is extravagant. Some papermakers

H

use the spent bleaching liquor, known as "back" bleach. The writer is of opinion that in natural fibres this is a mistake. In bleaching rags, very little bleach is required, because very little impurity is to be extracted, hence the spent liquor is of value, as it is not greatly polluted. A warm-bath might be used for a second person, but it greatly depends upon the state of the first person's hide. So it is with bleach liquor. As a rule in bleaching straw and esparto, the liquor used is exhausted. The pulp goes into the liquor brown or green, and comes out white. The bleach liquor is spent, and it is a mistaken notion to suppose that the saving of back bleach under such circumstances pays for the pumping, tank-room, and expenses of collection and use. There are various means used, indeed, to thoroughly exhaust the bleaching liquor, either by adding acid or heating with steam. For straw, probably the former is preferable, whilst heating undoubtedly suits esparto. The testing of bleaching powder should always be seen to, indeed as should the testing of all chemicals employed in a paper mill.

To the uninitiated, the change from a natural fibre to bleached pulp excites greater interest than any process in rag papermaking. The change is more distinct and more marvellous. The bleaching being ended, and the pulp in the beating engine, we have arrived at the same stage as where we halted in making paper from rags. It is now necessary to explain the process of making paper from the liquid in the beating engine. Before doing so, the reader must understand that in many instances the sizing, and colouring, and loading of the paper, are accomplished in the engine, and such papers are known as "engine-sized." To explain these operations will be our duty after considering the actual process of making a sheet of paper.

The method of making paper is at first sight very simple. Even, as in the various draining operations, perforated apparatus is used to allow the separation of the water from the pulp, so the actual production of a sheet of paper is accomplished by the same means. In the former case, the water was conducted away and left the pulp behind in mass; in this instance the water drains away in such a manner that only a thin film of pulp remains, and this thin film is the sheet of paper. This draining process is now effected both by hand and machinery; but for many years the hand process was the only one in operation. The hand process is a particularly interesting sight.

We must take up our position at the side of the vat containing the pulped or "beaten" rags, and we can trace the liquid pulp to the sheet of paper at one glance. The beaten pulp is kept constantly moving in the vat in order to prevent the solid fibrous matter settling, and thereby compromising the even density of the fluid pulp. A man dips a small square frame into the vat, gives it several peculiar motions with his hands, and passes the frame to a mate, who reverses it upon a "felt" or piece of woollen cloth like a blanket. Upon lifting the frame, a mass of pulp is seen upon the felt of the same shape and size as the frame. This sheet of pulp is covered immediately by another felt, and the frame again deposits a sheet of pulp, which is in turn covered by another felt, and so the process goes on until quite a pile of these pulp and felt sandwiches is obtained. They are then moved into a powerful press, hydraulic generally, and squeezed until as much water as possible is expelled. The felts are then removed, and the sheets of paper lay before us.

The frame is technically known as the "mould," and is really a sheet of fine wire cloth containing about 70 holes to the square inch. The wire is bound in a frame of hard wood and lays perfectly flat. Upon this, however, is a lid or framework top which fits the under sheet tightly, and leaves a small space between the woodwork base of the lower frame and that of the lid itself. When this lid is fitted the frame becomes really a mould having a perforated bottom. The pulp filling the mould drains itself, but is greatly assisted by the paper-maker, who, watching the settlement of the fibres upon the wire, gently inclines the mould to whatever direction he thinks fit to obtain a perfectly even deposition of fibre. To be able to effect this requires great skill and long experience, and so tenacious are the papermakers of their skill, that this art is an hereditary legacy, and descends from father to son. This is done to secure the business amongst a few men, who are in a position to wield all the power and sway belonging to mono

es.

This outline of the process is but a scanty reflection of the numberless details embodied in the successful art of paper-making. Skill is not only required by the papermaker and the others who help him and transmit the wet sheets through their processes of laying and pressing. The utmost care has to be taken in keeping the sheets clean and free from smears, and perhaps no factory ought to be cleaner than a paper mill. The standard of perfection is the one, or should be the one great aim of every papermaker, so far as cleanliness is concerned. Especially should this be the case in mills where expensive papers are made ; but in every mill a cleanly method is necessary, and there is no excuse whatever for that demoralisation of feeling which views a state of filth and dirt with indifference. The writer has seen numberless paper mills, and some have been models of condition, whilst pigs would have uttered a protest against a daily life in others. If low-classed papers be made, there is no reason why an accumulation of dirt is to accompany their manufacture. But in rag mills, where every sheet of paper wasted, and where every sheet of paper made is severely examined, cleanliness is a virtue of great price. Hence the floors are clean and kept swept with abundance of water, so that dust shall be unknown and specks absolute strangers.

To return to the mould. At this stage of the process of papermaking the watermark is introduced. It is quite unnecessary to enter into any discussion as to the age and origin of watermarks, but they are very interesting, and doubtless a great puzzle to many people. If a watermark be carefully observed, the paper is seen to be thinner and more transparent at the points where the mark extends. The designs of watermarks are countless, but they may be described as being of two characters, viz. : one to show the size of the sheet and the other for purely trade purposes. All hand-made papers, or papers made with moulds, are made to certain sizes, therefore the mark is not necessary as a distinction, though much used. Now, papermakers have their own names or some trade name for a watermark, and the way in which a watermark is inserted is extremely simple. The design is worked inversely upon the surface of the wire cloth. The design is of brass wire, and is sewn upon the cloth with very thin brass wire, which holds it tolerably firm. When the pulp settles and the sheet is pressed upon the felt, the wire design naturally compresses the pulp, making the sheet thinner by a degree corresponding with the body of the design. The compression of the pulp renders it more transparent, hence, wherever the design touches the pulp, the pulp when dried is more transparent than the rest of the sheet. Latterly an improved method of watermarking has been adopted. It consists of attaching the design to the wire cloth by a suitable metallic solder, which does away with the troubles that attend the unsewing or breaking of the wire thread employed in the old system.

The hand-made paper up to this stage is known as "water-leaf," or unsized paper. It will not do for writing paper yet; it is now, popularly speaking—blotting paper, and has to be sized to enable it to take ink. The sizing of paper is the rendering it impervious to moisture, so that it can be written upon without the same effects as follow an effort to write upon blotting paper. Before considering this feature, it will be well to consider the manufacture of paper by machinery.

The introduction of what might be termed the "paper machine" is veiled in uncertainty. Doubtless there were many ideas and many modifications of the machine before it was introduced to the trade. One of the first notions was a travelling procession of moulds. A few words in explanation of this machine will be interesting. In 1821 this peculiar machine was started at Springfield Paper Mills, near Edinburgh. It was a framework containing ten moulds, and they travelled upon a kind of railway of oval shape. The moulds were of various sizes so as to make the different sizes of hand-made paper. Whilst travelling a motion was given by peculiar mechanism to the moulds so as to imitate as closely as possible a hand-made papermaker's *modus operandi*. The moulds were supplied with pulp from the vat by a travelling strap, to which certain receptacles, shaped like a bucket, were affixed, and they tilted into each mould the necessary quantity of pulp for the size and substance of whatever sheet of paper had to be made. After the moulds had traversed a sufficient distance calculated to deprive the pulp of its water, they were, by a suitable apparatus, completely reversed upon a felt, which travelled also towards a pair of wet press or couch rolls. Here the sheets were couched, and on coming from the rolls were carried forward upon a long travelling felt clear of the machine, and were stacked in the ordinary way ready for the press.

This machine was patented and erected at the above mills, as an antidote to the strikes among the hand-made papermakers. The workpeople nick-named this machine the " wooden man." The patent was subsequently re-adjusted and improved for the construction of a second machine, but all the patents, plans and drawings, &c., prepared for legal purposes, were lost in transmission to London, and never have been found. The original drawings, however, will be shown in the Exhibition, and are the property of Messrs. George and William Bertram, of Edinburgh.

The great objection to this machine was the inability to go at any speed, as in rounding the curves at either end of the oval, the jerk was apt to pitch some pulp out of the moulds. However, the new patent that was lost was going to rectify this, by making the moulds travel straightforward and dip at the end, as an endless belt would do, and as a machine wire does now. At the present day this very idea is embodied in the mill in France, where the Bank of France notes are made. The exactly-similar machine of travelling vats is in use for making these notes, and another such machine is being erected for making the notes for the Bank of St. Petersburgh. Paper made by these machines, it is hardly necessary to state, was of first class quality, and closely resembled hand-made in every respect.

In the following year the Fourdrinier machine was introduced, and carried out the idea of the previous machine with more scope and surer speed. The first machines ended at the press rolls, and only produced the paper in a wet web; afterwards drying cylinders were introduced, and such improvements added as the papermaker now looks for in the modern paper machine.

The Fourdrinier paper machine is a very complicated piece of mechanism. The real ideas embodied in the machine itself comprise the mould, the felt, the press and the drying arrangement in one. The mould is represented by an endless wire, some 30ft. to 40ft. long, and of varying width from 48in. to 120in. and even 130in., according to requirement. In the early days of the paper machine, the wire was, of course, the main feature, as it, perhaps, is at the present time. When we consider that the great art of hand-papermaking combines the handling of the mould, guided by human hands and suggested by human intelligence ; a quick eye ever ready to supplement a deficiency or remedy a defect, and all the advantages to be obtained from a long experienced expert ; when we consider this,· and then compare the replacement of this live agency by a mere machine, we can begin to conceive the nice and delicate points the engineer has to contend with. The wire has to travel so that a perfect sheet of paper be produced ; the exodus of the water must be accomplished in a perfect and regular manner, for there is nobody to help or assist ; the paper must go through the rolls to be couched at an uniform speed and with uniform pressure, and the after-journey of the sheet is beset with many possible dangers, which the ingenuity of the engineer has to provide against in the machine.

A very important feature in a machine is the arrangement of felting. Papermakers' felts are very expensive articles, and are made by five manufacturers, who do all that capital and energy can for the papermaker. Felts are endless woollen bands of the same width as the machine ; they convey the paper to the rolls and cylinders, acting not only as leaders and guides, but assisting to dry the paper as it goes forward. In a paper machine there are numerous bearings, rollers, and other fittings, all of which contribute to the one grand result—success. A good machine is perfectly fitted in all senses, and will work without trouble, without stop, and without murmur. Like most mechanical appliances to replace querulous labour, the paper machine is always undergoing modifications with a view to improve a substitute for hand labour ; but the great principle is the same always, viz., to make a good sheet of paper.

An engine of from 15 to 20 horse-power, cylinders 15in. diameter and 2ft. 3in. stroke, condensing or high pressure, will

drive the couch rolls, one or two pairs of press rolls, intermediate and finishing calenders, pumps for pulp, back-water
and suction, and all the back gearing of a machine. The
average machine may be taken at 84 inches in width, with
15 cylinders, 4 feet in diameter, and the total weight of all,
including gearing, may be taken at about 75 tons. Such a
machine has to have the most stable foundations, brick, concrete or stone. In some places abroad, oak is used for foundations. The roof of a machine-room must be provided with
heating arrangement, as the steam from the cylinders would
otherwise condense and drip: the falling drops of water, it is
scarcely necessary to add, would make holes in the paper. The
steam ascending to the roof is always allowed to escape by
specially constructed ventilators to aid this object in every way.

The foregoing sketch of the paper machine must suffice,
and we will now return to the beating engine, where the pulp
is ready to be made into paper. It is for that purpose conducted to vats—called in a machine mill " stuff chests "—where
the pulp is constantly agitated by steam agitators. In some
instances, when rougher fibres than rags are used, fibres such
as straw, esparto, wood pulp, jute, &c., the pulp requires
cleansing before going to the machine, and for this purpose
passes to the "knotters." These machines all act upon one
and the same principle: it is the filtering of the pulp through
the knotter-plate, a bed of brass containing exceedingly fine
slits, just large enough to allow the thin, fine pulp to run
through, and keeping large pieces, grit, or any matters calculated to spot or speck the paper. Knotters, like every other
mechanical appliance, are made of all kinds of modifications of
one and the same idea. Some knotters contain the pulp, and
are shaken violently, so as to facilitate straining. Other
knotters rotate in a tank, into which the pulp runs. In these
knotters the outer plates allow the pulp to pass through, and
the hollow knotter conducts it to the machine. Other modifications exist, but suffice it to say, their object is exactly the
same, viz., to clear the pulp of grit and deleterious matter.

From the knotters, the pulp runs upon the machine, and is
perfectly liquid when it reaches the wire. The wire being gently

shaken, and swayed from side to side, imitates the hand paper-maker, and settles the pulp on its surface, leaving the water to run away. As the wire is constantly moving forward, the sheet of paper goes with it. It is prevented from overrunning by an india-rubber strap, about 1½in. square at each side, which moves upon the face of the wire and contributes to forming an edge. This is called the "deckle-strap." The paper, passing along over the suction-boxes, which by drawing air through the pulp help to dry it, reaches the wet-press, or couch-rolls, the bottom one of which serves to guide and drive the wire on its return journey. These rolls squeeze more moisture from the sheet of tender paper. The sheet proceeds to the dry-presses—either one or two pairs of rolls, where it is further squeezed, and its surface consolidated; hence it goes to the drying-cylinders. These hollow drum-shaped cylinders are heated by steam, and each dries the paper, which traverses round one to the other, being exposed to as mnch heated surface as possible. Some of these cylinders have felts running against their surfaces, to make the paper travel with an even surface, and to assist drying. In course of time, having traversed a sufficient number of hot cylinders, the paper passes over a cold cylinder, which is used to extract the electricity, and is reeled upon a roller at the end of the machine in an endless length, if no accident occur to to break the paper in its journey.

No description can give any adequate idea of a paper machine. It must be seen and explained when moving, and everybody who can should see this, without doubt, very beautiful and marvellous product of ingenuity.

The sizing of paper is the addition of some substance to the pulp or paper, which shall, as it were, shield each fibre with an impervious coating. In all good papers animal size is used. This is made from the best hide cuttings, and perhaps the best definition of size for a good paper is the best calves' feet jelly minus flavouring material. The size used in common papers is made from rosin. This is boiled with alkali until it saponi-fies. The mass is then carefully washed and boiled in clean water. This solution in combination with alum sizes the paper, coating each fibre with a thin film of an impenetrable chemical substance, the name of which is quite unfamiliar, and therefore of no use to the general world. The stage at which this sizing process is done differs, however, in the case of the several grades of paper. In common papers, the alum is put into the engine, then the rosin, then the colouring matter, and the whole goes to the machine, and the paper is reeled at the machine in a perfect condition, except as to being made ready for sale.

In the better classes of paper, however, there are several other methods. The term "tub-sized" is a common one now, and signifies that the paper is first made and then sized afterwards. Formerly, the animal size was dissolved in a tub, and each sheet was separately dipped by hand. This is done in some mills to this day. But there is an apparatus consisting of a travelling strap, that carries with it the sheets of paper, and taking them through the size delivers them at a roller, squeezes out the excess of size, the latter running back to the tub again. The sheet is then taken away and suspended in the centre over cowhair drying lines in a suitable room. Such papers are known as "tub-sized" and "loft-dried." In other instances the sheet of web or continuous paper is sized on the machine during its transit. The paper is conducted through a wooden tray of size, and goes over drying cylinders as usual to the end of the machine. In the case of common papers, this process of intermediate sizing is sometimes done, but starch is used in place of size. This or gum is added to give the paper weight; it is only done in some special kinds of paper.

As a rule, which will hold good in a practical sense, the best papers are tub-sized and loft-dried; the medium qualities are machine-sized with animal size, and the lower qualities are engine-sized and sized with rosin.

We may now consider paper made. It is utterly impossible to condense a hand-book upon papermaking into so small a space as this article affords. To every papermaker, the writer offers a humble apology for all omissions and the scant justice such a condensed account can but afford. A few words upon the "finishing" of paper will end this portion of our subject.

When the paper is taken from the drying loft it is rolled, and if a very fine surface be required, it is "glazed." In putting a very fine surface upon paper, a great pressure is what is required. Each sheet of paper is sandwiched with a copper or zinc plate, and heavily rolled between very powerful rolls. This gives a splendid surface. To obtain paper smooth upon one side and rough upon the other, two sheets of paper are rolled, when the sides next the metal will be found to be smooth, the insides remaining rough. Papers are often "friction glazed." The machine is composed of three rolls, the under one being of large diameter to sustain the weight and give the speed to the middle roll, also of large diameter, and covered with either cotton or paper, so as to form a bed for the paper being glazed. The top or friction roll is made of iron, generally chilled metal, and is very highly polished so as to impart a smooth and even surface to the paper. According to the glaze required in the paper this roll is driven at a corresponding speed over and above the speed of the paper, which is accomplished by an arrangement of wheelwork. This is a single glazing machine, but there are others which are composed of a larger number of rolls. The width of the machine varies somewhat, although the paper glazed by this method is never very wide. These papers are better glazed in the web than in sheet, for obvious reasons.

The examination of paper in the mill is conducted in the "salle," a large room, where girls overhaul every sheet, picking out all imperfections and torn sheets. The paper is then counted out into reams of 480, 500, or 516 sheets, and is then ready for the market. There are some exceptions, however, notably in Writings, which are often cut and made into packets of five quires, and in News for journals. This latter is not cut from the machine but reeled in a continuous sheet, and is sent in that condition to the printing office. In the case of machine-made paper, the rolls from the machine are cut into sheets. This is effected by machines which can cut several sheets at one time from as many rolls. A revolving knife, which can be set to cut any size, divides the paper from the several rolls, and little boys or girls can receive and stack at the end of the machine. There are numbers of cutting machines for paper mills, but it is beyond our space to particularize.

When the sheets are passed and counted into reams, they are sometimes "folded," otherwise they are sold "flat." They are put up in wrappers, string, and duly labelled, weighed and dispatched to their destination. News is sent away in reels and is sold by weight. If in reeling the web breaks, the paper is glued, and all such sheets in the printing office are rejected and their weight deducted.

When writing paper has to be delivered in packets, each sheet is cut into four and folded, every twenty-four sheets making a quire, and five quires going to every packet. These papers are sold by the ream, and retail by the packet. News is sold at per pound weight, and invoices for several tons are by no means uncommon. In machine-made common papers, nearly all business is conducted by weight, and only in the best classes is the paper sold as in hand-made, by the ream. A ream of paper for the printer contains 516 sheets in England, 500 in Scotland. A ream always contains one of three numbers of sheets, viz. 500, 516, or 480, but there are many sizes and weights. Indeed, a ream of machine-made paper can be made to any size; but there are certain recognized sizes of paper in the trade, such as posts, crowns and double crowns; demys, and double demys; royals, caps, &c., &c. The size of a paper is ascertained by measuring the length and breadth and quoting the two dimensions. Thus a double crown is 20 by 30, and a royal 20 by 25, and so on. This means that a sheet of double crown size paper is 30 in. long and 20 in. wide. The weight is also added, and testifies to the weight of a ream of sheets of that particular size.

Wrapping and brown papers are made in the same way as their betters, with rougher materials and workmanship generally. The general character of brown papers is so well known as not to necessitate any description here; but it may be noticed that they exemplify an excellent use of waste materials in clearing away old rope, bagging, tarpaulin, odds and ends, and all fibrous rubbish worthless for any other class of paper. There are, however, many wrapping papers of high quality for toughness and durability, and upon which much trouble and expense are lavished.

To produce paper with economy and efficiency, a well found mill is required, and many of the public are but little aware of the immense capital and brain power necessary to carry on a paper mill. In addition to all the machinery mentioned, there are the large buildings to hold it; boilers to provide steam; a tall chimney for the boilers; boilers for fibre; stationary engines for pumping, for there must be an inexhaustible supply of water; and, finally, there must be a powerful driving power with fittings complete. In some mills hydraulic presses and filter beds, dams, and water machinery are also necessary. In short, a papermaker's art requires money, intelligence, skill, and perseverance, qualities which, when the public examine the products, they will ungrudgingly allow the manufacturers.

Paper can be classified as follows :—

Hand-made Papers.

Account Book, Bank Note, Bank Post, Drawing, Loan, Writings, Parchment.

Machine-made Papers. (First class, from rags only).

Account Book, Bank Note, Bank Posts, Blottings, Bowl, Chart, Drawing, Loan, Writings, Plate.

Machine-made Papers. (Medium, rags and esparto or jute).

Account Book, Blottings, Cartridges, Drawings, Music, Plate, Printings, Writings, Tissues.

Machine-made Papers. (Common, straw, wood and bagging).

Blottings, Cartridges, Collar Papers, Copyings, Long Elephants, Middles, News of all kinds, Printings, Small Hands, Writings (common), Railway Buffs, Telegrams.

Machine-made Papers. (Browns, &c.)

Blue Groceries, Browns, Casings, Glazed Casings, Mill Wrappers, Purples, Royal Hands, Skips, Small Caps, Starch, Tips, &c.

Uncommon and Special Papers.

Bowl Papers—Made from finest material. The sheets are perforated in the centre and threaded upon a spindle, afterwards submitted to hydraulic pressure. By this means a roller is built up of such hardness as to rival chilled steel. These bowls are used in glazing calicoes and papers.

Cheque Papers.—Made by hand from the best rags. These papers are chiefly noticeable for an elaborate water-mark. Used for cheques and bank drafts.

Boards.—Made by hand, with one or two exceptions. Made from rope, jute, and other similar strong materials, and used for bookbinding, pressing, &c.

Linear Papers.—All papers containing lines to guide writing. The lines are a watermark.

Parchment.—Made by hand of finest materials, and the paper is coated in dilute sulphuric acid, which gives the paper its peculiar appearance.

S.O. Papers. (Stationery Office Papers).

Hand-made papers are highly esteemed, and properly so, for their excellent properties of strength, durability, and body. In the process of manufacture, the fibres, never being subjected to sudden contraction or expansion, but being allowed to arrange themselves naturally, greater strength seems to be the result, and it is found that hand-made papers will undoubtedly last longer than any others. The edges of a hand-made paper do not possess the regularity of a machine-made, and are known as deckle-edged. These rough edges afford a capital test of the paper. The main features of a hand-made paper are the watermark, the substance, feel, strength, and sizing of the paper.

All hand-made papers are made and sold to regular sizes, and each size has its own regular weight. The paper is sold at per ream in all cases. Colours—cream, yellow and blue. The next papers in quality to hand-made are the tub-sized and loft-dried varieties, and it is extremely difficult to detect one from the other, so perfect are the appliances of the paper machine. The manufacture of these papers is directed towards as near an approach as possible to hand-made papers. Owing to their careful handling in manufacture, these papers possess all the good features of a hand-made, even to the watermark. These papers can be made to any size or weight, but the latter are generally guided by the demand for letter or note sizes in writings. The ream is 480 sheets and is perfect, there being no " outsides."

The strongest specimen of paper in the world, a £5 note, is a hand-made paper, but it is very difficult to excel the bank-note paper now made by machine, and there are many people who prophecy the days when hand-made papers shall be no more. Without discussing this question, there is no doubt that a machine possesses every advantage over any number of vats. It is more regular in results, and does not strike for higher wages or the attainment of any frivolous object.

The great consumer of paper is the printer. Though hand-writing and the use of the pen and pencil consume an enormous quantity of paper, printing and its huge appliances are the great customer of the papermaker.

When we consider the Press, the bookseller, the railway companies and other large printing communities, we must allow that type blackens more paper than the human hand. Printing papers can be had and made to order, of all sizes, weights and colours ; of all qualities and prices also. A printer requires more kinds of paper than any other consumer, as he has to do such varied work, requiring great varieties of paper. The printer objects to clay in his paper, and there is now very little excuse for clay being in paper. The use of wood pulp is cheaper in the end and makes a better paper. Every printer should insist upon the cry, " no-clay." Papermakers might have to raise their prices, but printers would save their type and produce better work, worth more money.

Wrapping papers are very extensively used. In these days, every purchaser requires his goods to be wrapped up in a piece of paper, and the shopkeeper has to buy paper. For shop use, several special papers are made, i.e., blues and purples for sugar. Tips are for sugar, skips also ; there are special papers for butter, tea and flour ; the drapers delight in small hands, and iron-mongers will find papermakers study their special wants. Large quantities of paper are made for bags of all kinds. Long elephants are made to adorn the walls of our houses, whilst even pins and needles have a special wrapping paper of their own. Paper is specially made for starch and cigarettes.

Readers may have noticed a class of papers called "middles." These papers are for making cardboard, and will be alluded to under cards in No. 11 of this article. Middles are generally inferior papers, but as they have to be manufactured with goods which have a high value, they are required to possess their own particular good points as to colour and surface.

The colour of paper deserves a few words. Pure paper has a cream colour, hence the word " cream " note. White paper owes its dazzling and brilliant tone to the admixture of a little blue in the engine, which imparts life to the colour. " Blue" is a distinct colour of that shade, as opposite to " yellow," which in the papermaker's world is often blue. A yellow wove is what the outer world would decidedly call blue. This apparent fallacy has its origin in an anecdote, which could not, however, be very well introduced here. These are the three great shades of paper ; all others are specially made to order.

Many people do not understand the difference between a " wove " and a " laid " paper. Essentially there is no difference at all, so far as the quality of the paper goes. The appearance of a writing depends upon the " dandy roll " used. The dandy is a hollow skeleton roll of brass, covered with a wire, containing the water-mark. The dandy is fixed over the wire, and runs upon the web paper, impressing upon it the counterpart of its design or mark. In " wove " papers a dandy with plain wire is used, hence the paper is plainly marked. In " laid " papers the dandy leaves the peculiar ribbed imprint which a laid paper possesses, an imprint of longitudinal thin lines and horizontal thicker lines. The surface of a laid paper is therefore rather rougher than a wove paper. Sometimes if the dandy be old, the lines are scarcely visible ; this is not very frequent, so that the uninitiated can always detect a laid paper by holding it before the light. If quite plain, it is a " wove ; " if it contains light column lines running the length of the sheet, with fainter ones at right angles, it is a " laid."

There are about 400 paper mills at work in the United Kingdom, and about 30 to 40 others unoccupied. Of these, by far the largest proportion are brown paper mills, and the next being printings and news. Lancashire is very celebrated for its large mills, whilst Kent is also famous for its paper mills and good paper. Many of the southern mills are renowned for their beauty, and the papermaker's occupation is often wistfully envied. Besides the proprietor, who generally is not only a hard worker, but an enthusiast in his business, there is a working staff in most mills, consisting of manager, engineer, foreman, night foreman, fitters, papermakers and labourers. Generally speaking, every papermill is well organized so far as system and management go. Every department will be found to have its own staff ; while an office and counting-house conduct the monetary affairs.

The uses of paper are more or less well known and will be, so far as the public are concerned, described in the next chapter on Stationery. A few remarks upon the present state of the Paper Trade will close this Essay.

During the past six or seven years the value of paper has steadily fallen, until it is now a moot question as to whether certain classes of paper are worth making at all. This condition of things has arisen simply from an over-eagerness to supply a cheap article. This desire created severe competition, and a down-hill race commenced, which has been prosecuted with bitter energy and headlong speed ; and now the competitors find themselves at the bottom, exhausted, with no solatium or prize, and a weary journey back. There has been a sad amount of reckless and utterly insane anxiety to provide cheap paper to a public who never asked for it, who never desired it, and who, when they have it, grumble at and are ashamed of it. Moreover, the foreigners stepped in, and have not only maintained the hold given to them, but have actually lowered prices, and are at this day cutting against us successfully in catering for our great London daily press. Meanwhile, raw materials, as was instanced in November, are subject to sudden and unexpected fluctuations, being bought up in America, and leaving our papermakers unprovided with the wherewithal to work. Altogether, the trade is in a bad state.

Until the unnecessary and stupid policy of deteriorating the market be abandoned, paper will never rise again. So long as stocks are kept up, and papermakers supply men to undersell

I

each other, trade cannot improve. It is a lamentable fact that some papermakers are making paper for drapers to sell at under trade prices, and for co-operative stores to do the same. Further, papermakers will offer paper at something lower than their neighbour to secure the order. The process of offering lower and lower goes on until personal feeling will prompt a price that will cause an actual loss even to the maker. This is not business. This is not the kind of commerce that has made England what she is, and the paper trade what it was. There must be an end to this, and that end must be disaster. This "throat-cutting" policy is ruining the trade and the country; for, independent of profits, a lower price necessitates lower quality. Lower quality is the stepping-stone to an equality with our inferiors, with whom we must eventually, with whom we have been compelled to compete. Let the trade think over this, weigh it carefully, and see what can be done. It is a matter for personal consideration. If every papermaker would resolve upon a limit, and work half-time, or stay the ruinous lowering of price and quality in the best way he can, prices would rise. A general union seems to be impossible, because there is no personal regard or confidence. One mill cannot make all the cheap paper, nor can half-a-dozen. If the trade, as a body, refuse to sell at lower than a certain margin, and allow nothing to tempt them below, matters will improve.

(Copyright.)

No. II.—STATIONERY.

By W. F. Catcheside.

It is quite as difficult to define the single word " stationery " as it is to accurately define the word " paper." Both cover an immense area, which, as time goes on, seems to increase until really there appears to be no boundary whatever to the field covered by either paper or stationery. Anybody from the outer world and unused to the atmosphere and influences of this special trade would consider stationery " writing-paper and envelopes." Some more comprehensive minds would include " and all similar things." This phrase would comprise all the apparatus and materials used in conjunction with writing-paper and envelopes. As this is a popular view, attention must be given to it, and non-commercial readers will soon be disabused not only of the exclusive character of stationery, but they will find that " writing-paper and envelopes " are in themselves no mean business.

It is extremely difficult to give a correct meaning for " stationery." Many goods sold by a " stationer " are certainly not stationery, nor indeed have they anything whatever to do with stationery. To wit—medicines, portmanteaux, leather bags, jewellery, and a host of other similar goods are not stationery proper in the strict sense of the trade, so far as the writer's opinion goes. It would be well here to observe that any statements in the form of opinions are only personal, and merely those of one individual, who would be sorry to dictate or behave in any way egotistically to the trade either generally or personally.

That stationery is, as it were, an inanimate world governed by paper, the author feels will be generally acknowledged. It seems quite impossible to keep paper out of our minds when stationery is under consideration. But there are undoubtedly other forms of stationery which go beyond paper and all apparatus used in its consumption by human beings themselves. We all know that to be able to use writing-paper and envelopes we must have pencils or pens and ink, receptacles for all these utensils, perhaps sealing-wax, wafers, or gum; maybe we require a ruler, and some of us cannot do without a blotting-pad, pen-wiper, pen-rack, copying-book and press. There, at once, is a leap from paper pure and simple!

But a sub-division might be made of our subject, which the author, in all modesty, thinks might be accepted.

The first might be called " manugraphic stationery," and would appertain entirely and solely to the popular view of stationery, viz., writing materials inclusive.

The second let us call " typographic stationery," which would embrace the union of printing and paper in all its various forms and modifications. This sub-division would have an exclusive character in one way, it would only embrace the union of the two great trades, so far as artistic and ornamental, or perhaps fanciful or luxurious combination goes. A newspaper is a combination of printing and paper; but is it stationery? All printers must use paper, and therefore, so far as the combination is concerned, no line could be drawn except at the point ornamental or luxurious, and for the present, to prevent confusion, such a sub-division might be allowed.

The original interpretation of a " stationer " is, " one who kept a shop or stall." In olden days, it would appear, trading was extensively carried on by hucksters or pedlers, who went over the country selling their goods, much in the same way as they do in the bye-country places to-day. Now it is probable, as towns increased in size, that some of the hucksters who had accumulated money opened stalls and became stationary or immoveable traders. Perhaps, in time, they were called " stationers." This term would, as the dictionaries inform us, apply thus to all shopkeepers; but the question arises, how did the general term " stationer " stick to this one particular trade, which in our days retains the old name of multitude? This may be explained, perhaps, in this way:—Many " stationers " became such because they found their goods too cumbersome to carry about. It is well known that in olden times books were sold at stalls. By-and-bye these booksellers would become associated with one peculiarity, viz., their shop or stall, hence they would be called. stationers. To this day "bookseller and stationer" is a common title of trade, and the two trades of books and stationery are nearly always closely and intimately associated.

In 1493 the Stationers' Company was instituted, under the government of a master and two wardens. The company was composed then of the writers of the religious books, pamphlets, &c., who congregated in the district now known as Paternoster Row, a name doubtless originating from these writers. The Stationers' Company received their first Charter from Queen Mary, 1556, under the title of "The Master and Keepers, or Wardens, and Commonalty, of the Mystery or Art of the Stationers of London." At this time printers seem to have been the active parties in the company, judging from the signatures to the deed of Charter.

This Charter was renewed in 1588 by Queen Elizabeth, amplified in 1684 by Charles II., and confirmed in 1690 by William and Mary. At the present time the Stationers' Company occupies a high position in the guilds of the City of London; but they might do very much more for the trade than they do. The question of copyright, and the serious inconveniences and losses it occasions to publishers here, is a matter surely for the consideration of the company.

Let us take, without further delay, our first sub-division in hand, and treat of

MANUGRAPHIC STATIONERY.

Undoubtedly the chief article consumed under this heading is paper, and the following may be taken as a tolerably full list of papers recognised in the provision of writing materials:— Writings, envelope papers, blottings, ledger and account-book papers, carbon and manifold, tissue and tracings, copyings, and metallic note-papers.

In the former part of this article devoted to paper, the manufacture of these papers generally was described; but in dealing first with writings, it may be said that in these days any paper can be a writing. It is, therefore, rather puzzling to describe a writing beyond saying that it is a paper sold in quires and packets of certain sizes. This broad definition will cover the whole question.

Writings can be bought of any quality and any shade of colour; but the sizes are not so variable. In buying writings the stationer may prefer to fold and packet the paper himself; in this case he buys the paper flat or in folio. The flat sheet is cut into four, making quarto sheets; these are then folded, making what is known as octavo. If this sheet be folded it becomes a 16mo.

The value of a writing depends not so much upon the paper itself as upon the taste of the writer. Some people prefer a smooth surface, highly glazed; some prefer exactly the opposite, a coarse, rough, uneven surfaced paper; others like the happy medium. Steel pens as a rule will write more easily upon a very smooth surface than a rough one The rough papers have been called the "ploughed field" series, a name in all senses appropriate.

The fancies or flights of popular feeling which are created or appealed to by writing papers are most curious. Almost violent controversies occur respecting the claims of writing papers. The old question of "laid" and "wove" papers often occasions bitter dispute. Taking everything into consideration, a medium surfaced laid paper is the best material for a writing for ordinary purposes. For what may be called fancy stationery, there are numberless varieties of papers; but amongst the most popular are repps and their modifications. The repp papers are most extensively used and are made in all tints and colours, some of which are excessively ugly. The repp mark is produced by rolling the plain paper between heavy rolls bearing the pattern of the repp. "Satin" and "damask" patterns are produced by the same means. The repps are made in all qualities, from very cheap to very expensive papers. Linear papers contain a waterline for the guidance of people who cannot write straight across the sheet.

The nomenclature of writings is of interest. The types of writings known as cream woves and laids, azure do., antiques, vellums, originals, old styles, and a host of other names, have certain slight characteristics which, perhaps it may be said, are known only to the largest wholesale stationers. There is very little to choose between many of them. Note papers are, however, susceptible of names without end. Popularity is reflected by trade names, and all public characters must ever remember that one penalty of fame is to be immortalised in the label of a five-quire packet of note paper.

We must get on with our subject. Writings exist at from 4d. to 2s. per lb., and to the shame of the trade these two papers can both be called writings. Even as there are good, bad, and indifferent writers, it would seem that material is provided to suit their several degrees of proficiency. In buying writing paper the average public should never give less than 2s. per packet, and leave the low classed and cheap writings to the humbler and poor classes for whom they were, doubtless, made by some self-sacrificing paper maker. Writings should always be good, and stationers would do well throughout the country to restore the trade to its proper level, and discourage in every possible way the descent to the use of common writing paper. Whilst the enterprise in bringing out novel designs in writing papers is worthy of all praise, the public should never be invited by the trade to favour cheap goods. Good writing papers cannot be made to sell at less than 9d. per lb., and the public should know that when they buy the cheap packets they are buying rubbish.

Envelopes are merely writing papers in a special form. They can be made of the same paper as note, and can therefore match the latter exactly. There are many ingenious machines for making envelopes, a process which will be fully illustrated in the Exhibition. The manufacture of envelopes necessitates a liberal use of machinery. First there are steel knives to cut out the shapes. These are then fed to a machine which folds, gums, stamps and counts them in one continuous operation. In most instances the envelope machine is self-feeding also. The details of envelope making are too numerous for full explanation here, but suffice it to say that the making of an envelope means a large outlay of mechanical and brain power. Black edging, for mourning stationery, is done by hand. Girls range the envelopes or note in long rows, each sheet overlapping its neighbour. With a rule to guide the margin, the girl rubs a brush, containing the black, over the edges, and the drying completes the operation.

There has been much fantastic display evinced in the various shapes of envelopes. All sorts of sizes and shapes have been, are, and probably will continue to be invented. We have had very long and narrow, very broad and wide ; but to all intents and purposes the two popular sizes are letter and court sizes; the former for general and the latter for ladies' use. The advantage of a court envelope is not very great. It is true that it is only necessary to double the paper once for this envelope; but as business men hardly ever fold their letters themselves, nd as ladies' time will allow them to dispense with clerks, the apparent boon of the court envelope is shrouded in mystery.

Blotting paper is paper without sizing material. It is made chiefly in the following colours :—pink, white, blue, yellow and mauve, other tints being scarce. The main characteristics of good blotting paper are its absorbent nature and a thick feel. It is sold at per lb., and in reams. It can be had of any size or weight according to order.

Copyings are the varieties of paper used for taking the imprint of letters, and are only known in offices and counting houses. These papers are really very thin blottings, but are not suited for the same purpose as thick blottings, being very fragile. They can be made of almost any quality, and are sold at per lb., or ream.

Tissues and tracing papers are frequently used in the office or for educational use; the former for preservative purposes, and the latter for tracing, a process much in vogue amongst architects and engineers. The tracing paper is transparent, so that the outline of a drawing can be transferred without the trouble of a free-hand or mechanical drawing from sight. They are very useful indeed, and can be had of all large wholesale stationers.

Drawing papers are a heavy stock and item with the stationer. They are made of the best material, and are used very largely by almost all communities, either for pleasure or pastime. The chief characteristics of a good drawing paper are the following, viz.: thickness and good substance, good sizing, uniformity of substance and a kind colour not too dazzling. The hand-made varieties are more highly prized, but machine-made imitate very closely all the features of their superiors. The following are the sizes in use :—

DRAWING PAPERS.—(Sizes and Weights.)

	in.		in.			
Emperor ...	72	×	48	...	...	620lbs.
Antiquarian	53	×	31	...	...	250 ,,
Double Elephant	40	×	26¾	...	...	130 ,,
Atlas ...	... 34	×	26	...	...	98 ,,
Columbier	... 34½	×	23¼	...	...	102 ,,
Imperial	... 30	×	22	,..	...	72 ,,
Elephant	... 28	×	23	...	...	72 ,,
Super Royal	... 27	×	19	...	...	54 ,,
Royal ...	... 24	×	19	...	...	44 ,,
Medium	... 22	×	17½	...	...	34 ,,
Demy ...	... 20	×	15¼	...	...	25 ,,
Large Post	... 20¾	×	16¾	...	...	23 ,,
Post ...	... 19	×	15¼	...	...	20 ,,
Foolscap	... 17	×	13½	...	...	15 ,,
Pott ...	... 15	×	12½	...	...	10 ,,
Copy ...	... 20	×	16	...	...	20 ,,

Account-book papers are also used very largely in manugraphic stationery, and are indeed necessary fittings of an office. The manufacture of account books is a business of its own, and would occupy far too much space to induce any attempt at description. The best account books contain the best paper naturally. It must stand scratching out, the wear and tear of daily reference, the test of time, frequent trials of other severe nature, and has to be particularly well sized to bear red and other coloured inks. What applies to the paper is equally applicable to the binding, so that a good account book is a very first class article and requires all that skill and money can do. When it is understood that cheap imitations are produced, it can also be understood that account books vary from good to bad in all the stages of inferiority suggested by modern improvements and progress. A good account book is like a good sheet of writing paper—a specimen of skill and beauty; the former illustrating man's highest attainments; the latter depicting sterling worth and purity of work and material. The cheap account book is an effort to lead the public to regard the above virtues as an unnecessary expense, but honours their superiority by as close an imitation and as deceitful a result as possible.

Such may be termed a very terse summary of the papers required by a stationer for manugraphic use. Other papers may be kept, and a general assortment of printings, such as demys, double demys, double crowns, &c., will be found needful. In all cases the retailer will find it is the best policy to deal with a large wholesale stationer. Some prefer sending to the paper mill. This is also in some instances preferred by the mill. As a rule, however, a wholesale stationer has a general stock, and plenty of it; has facilities for opening out small accounts, which would be a worry at a mill; and has travellers, and altogether further appliances for serving the retailer than a paper mill. As to the question of money, it is a question whether a wholesale stationer's account is not much more to the liking of a mill than a dozen pettifogging, dubious customers. These remarks are merely intended to dispel the notion that a paper mill can benefit to any serious extent by opening out accounts, and doing a direct trade. A papermaker's duty is to keep his name, mill, and special papers well before the trade, so that his stationer shall not be "a stranger in the land," and be compelled to introduce his principal wherever he shows his samples.

It is not necessary to enter into any details as to how paper is sold. As a rule, the wholesale stationer will always oblige his customer, not only in quantities of paper, but in payment for the same. All such matters are arranged, and are not dependent upon any custom or usance of trade.

To help us write or depict character on paper—why not say, to use paper?—we must have pens and ink. To use pens and ink we require racks, wipers, &c., and in a moment we can scan an entire office completely fitted up for the purpose solely of using paper.

The history of pens is a long one, but an interesting one. A pen, from its very common nature, is apt to be looked down upon, but the production of a pen requires a great capital, a great factory, and a great amount of intelligence. Birmingham shafts and their smoke testify to this, for the steel pen trade is a great feature of the great midland town. Steel pens are comparatively modern luxuries. The old quill pen is still used to a great extent for some reason, which may owe its existence to the fact that the people who use quill pens have the time and amiability to mend them. A steel pen is made from strips of steel about 2½-in. wide, and these strips are rolled until they are thin enough to be cut by a steel die, which stamps out the pen as a plain, flat piece of steel. This is then pierced and rounded, slit, polished, tempered, and examined, each operation requiring care, skill, and speed. The pens are made of all shapes, sizes, and colours by the process of cutting by dies. No more interesting sight can be seen, and no manufacture is carried on with more successful result, artistically speaking. Pens are also made of gold, but these are naturally very expensive. They have the great advantage of being unaffected by the acidity of inks, and may be, therefore, cheap in the long run.

Pens are made of bone and ivory, also vulcanite, but, practically speaking, the pen of the past was the quill, the present is the steel pen, whilst the pen of the future must be left to the fortune of Fate. America, the wondrous country of invention, has produced the stylographic pen, an instrument which carries its own supply of ink and is always ready. These pens seem destined to attract much more attention. Penholders are made of such numerous materials that it is scarcely worth while naming them ; but there are holders of wood of all kinds, metals of all kinds, glass, ivory, vulcanite, paper-stuff, bone, quills, &c., &c. These are to be had in all lengths and colours.

Next to pens come pencils, for manugraphic use. Pencils are very familiar objects with all of us. They are our schoolday companions, and we learn their use, perhaps, before any other of manugraphic manufacture. Slate pencils and slates are very useful articles, but are of too exclusive a nature to warrant many remarks. Slates have been greatly improved during the past few years, and are now made both light, durable, and economical. The pencils used for paper are of two kinds, black and coloured. The black lead pencil is the commoner one, and is extensively manufactured in Cumberland, where the graphic substance is found; indeed its name is graphite, from the use made of it. In ordinary pencils, a square piece of graphite, or lead, is encased with wood, chiefly cedar; but pocket pencils are made of every conceivable substance, bone, ivory, silver, gold, &c. In these cases the lead is a round mass, which, by suitable mechanical arrangements in the case, can be either protruded or withdrawn, as necessity requires. Pencils, indeed, are now made of all materials, all sizes, all shapes, and can be had at any cost whatever. It is a common practice now to ornament pencils with jewels and precious stones, so that no line can possibly be drawn as to the value or even nature of a pencil beyond its being a graphic instrument.

Manifold writing books are most convenient articles. They not only save the use and inconveniences of ink, but they give a copy of the graphic matter in additional. For portable use, a manifold writer is most convenient. The writing instrument is called a stylus, and is usually made of ivory. The carbon paper is of course black, but blue papers are also used. A companion in all senses is the manifold writer to travellers. It will carry paper and envelopes, stamps, and cards, and provide the writing materials and preserve a copy of everything written.

Chalks and crayons are used for the delineation of graphic character by hand, and are specially manufactured for their object. In all cases, pens and pencils are neatly " put up " by the maker, who does all he can to help their sale. Show cards and samples are freely used, and no business creates a greater display of enterprise than the one above alluded to. Pens in general are sold by the gross, some few exceptions being packed in dozens. The same applies to pencils.

Inks are writing fluids. They are in all cases chemical pro-ductions, and are made from sulphate of iron and nutgalls. Various modifications, additions, &c., are included in this very ambiguous receipt for ink, but practically these general ingredients form the mainstay of ordinary ink. Ink should not be too acid, otherwise it corrodes steel pens and renders them unfit for use. Ink should not thicken or deposit any settlement. It is not necessary that it should write very black; frequently light looking inks look blacker after some exposure to time and its influences than their blacker varieties. A little clove is a good addition to ink, assisting its preservation from fungus. If copying ink be made, a little gum is added.

Besides black, there are other coloured inks, notably red and blue. These coloured inks, however, are used almost entirely in the counting house, and by rulers of account books. Many fancy coloured inks have been introduced, notably violet and its various shades, but beyond a consumption amongst domestic servants and other humble persons, the coloured writing inks have very little sale.

Of late years the Graphs have come largely into use, and consist simply of a clever adaptation of the absorbent powers of glue and similar substances. A letter is written in a prepared graph ink upon paper, and the latter is pressed upon a sheet of gelatinous composition, which retains such a quantity of colouring matter, that as many as 150 copies can be taken from the surface by merely pressing as many clean sheets upon the composition. The saving of time in circulars and other similar work is immense, but until a black ink is invented, the graph will never come into universal use.

The office table requires many other adjuncts to complete an outfit for manugraphic operations. Inkstands are required, and who can describe the exact numbers and varieties of modern inkstands? Is not their name, legion? Then we have pen wipers and pen racks: the former have nearly disappeared. Ten or twenty years ago a penwiper was an article of *vertu*, a work of art, and an evidence of skill, combined with great tenderness of feeling when made for a present. Now, in these days, when the sampler, the book-marker, and many other products of our fair ancestors are no more, the penwiper has vanished from the scene. The circular, saw-edged, one-ivory-buttoned relic has seen its last day, and people of the year 1880

either grovel in an indifference which permits natural evapora-
tion on the pen, or stick their pens into a small brush upon the
office table.

Rulers are useful, especially for the clerks' office, as are also
scratching-out knives, erasers, india rubber, letter balances, and
every article which tends to promote order and methodical
habits. A word may be here said about sealing wax, gum, and
wafers. Sealing wax is an old-fashioned article, and seems to
be in some way connected with the seals we occasionally see
dangling from the " fob " of some ancient remnant of past ages.
But sealing wax has many uses beyond the one popularly known,
viz., to fasten letters. Perhaps the most general use of sealing
wax is for the securing of parcels and bottles. It is used for
this purpose not only as helping to secure a parcel, but the wax,
being able to take an impression, is a tell-tale as to the safe
transit of the parcel. In bottle wax, the seal acts also as
an advertisement. The qualities of good wax are, its colour
and its constancy of consistence in all climates. Bright,
brilliant wax is always good; but there are other coloured
waxes in use, which serve all the purposes of the most common
variety.

Wafers are decidedly old and out of date. They are used
occasionally in offices, and in the Colonies : the envelope, however, has almost if not entirely superseded them. Gum is the
product of a plant, and is too well known for any description
here. It is sold in solid form ; but for office use is put up
in bottles, either simple or fitted with a brush ready for use.
Gum is a most useful article in the office or house, and is a
safe article of stock. Very cheap bottles are sold ; but the
public would do well to pay a fair price and get a good article.
Although it would seem impossible to misunderstand so simple
a rule as this, yet the fact is people do not observe it in most
instances.

Before dismissing the general collective articles appertaining
strictly to the use of paper, it would be well to mention the
subject of ruling by machine. Several machines will be working
in the Exhibition, and it will be observed that a ruling machine
does manual work in far quicker time and with greater accuracy.

The methods by which this is accomplished, it is not the writer's wish to explain; he would rather leave the work actually performed to speak for itself.

Of late years stationers' sundries have become a distinct article in trade, and a few lines devoted to the subject must have place in this essay. Stationers' sundries may be described as the metal, wood and glass addenda to stationery. The leading lines are as follows:—Stationery cabinets of all kinds; inkstands, calendars, all appliances for letters, such as balances, delivery and post racks, files, clips, letter weights, and apparatus generally for arranging and safe custody of letters and papers; string-boxes and all such articles.

Stationery cabinets are neat wooden cases fitted with suitable compartments for note paper, envelopes, invoice forms, cards, pen trays, inkstand and bottle racks, &c. They can be made single or double so as to stand upon an office table and serve for two people. They are very useful, cheap, and very methodical, assisting in keeping order and comfort in any office. The letter appliances are also very useful and of inestimable benefit to an office.

Files are very good things in their way, and our American cousins have made them quite a study, and have produced almost elaborate systems for filing letters and papers. Files are really any apparatus for registering the receipt and date of receipt of letters and papers, and they may assume any shape or form according to inventive capacity.

Clips are useful to prevent the loss and straying of papers. Clips hold by a spring any reasonable number of sheets firmly, and as they can be at handy reach on the table, are very useful to all business men who have much correspondence. Boxes to hold letters for "post" or "delivery" are likewise good, and should be encouraged as contributing to order and method. Birmingham is noted as the depôt for stationers' sundries, their origin having emanated from that town. The most elaborate machinery is employed now in the preparation of these sundries, and economy is always strictly studied in their preparation for the market.

It is quite impossible to notice all the articles forming what are known as stationers' sundries, but the above will perhaps guide the retailer as to the goods necessary to tempt his customers. In these special goods, always keep in mind one grand thing, viz., novelty. Stationers' sundries are the butterflies of the trade. To-day they live, to-morrow they die. A good sharp man will always know what will "go," and upon his judgment depends the sale of many new goods. The best way for a retailer is to inspect the stock, and be thoroughly acquainted with every new thing of manufacturers, so that he can order at once and present a new thing to his customers. The general public like novelties, however short lived they may be, and buyers will often invest where their fancy is pleased in preference to steady selling articles.

Inkstands may now be reckoned among sundries. Of late years glass goods have crept into stationery to a considerable extent, and nothing prettier can be imagined than a cut-glass inkstand. It is clean and can always look nice and new. However, every month sees some new modification of inkstands in glass, and the only way for retailers to keep *au courant* with such novelties is to diligently study their trade journal. In its columns, provided it is a proper and respectable organ, they will see not only the drawings of the goods themselves, but notes and hints from capable judges to guide and help to form their own opinions. All trade journals strive to keep their readers well informed. Some have more success and greater influence than others : it is for the trade to select and judge for themselves.

Before finishing our heading "Manugraphic Stationery," let us pause a moment and glance at the old-fashioned forms of stationery—desks, escritoires and such preservers and receptacles of paper and writing materials. Desks, at one time, were doubtless highly prized, but in these days they are too cumbersome and too expensive. It is true that cheap desks are made, and are successful in many ways commercially, but the stationery cabinet has superseded the desk, being more handy and more ornamental in all respects. The main feature of a receptacle for stationery must be the ability to expose its entire contents at a glance, and thereby give no inconvenience to its owner. We verily live in an age of luxury. A desk in our days, except among school boys, is never seen. In business the cabinet and a slope, or inclined writing plane, are in vogue. The slope may be in the shape of a desk, that is, be hollow and contain papers. It may also be fitted with a blotting pad, and is thereby doubly useful. In some cases the top of the slope contains a calendar, which is a still further improvement. These slopes are made of a combination of wood, leather and straw or wood board ; are very durable, very convenient and cheap in the bargain. It is not our desire to say anything against desks. Far from it. Let our readers remember we are dealing with modern stationery, and we give in our remarks modern views, gathered from an experience of modern tastes and usages.

There are a few other manugraphic articles which assist us, and are of daily, if not hourly, use in business. For instance, who could be without a pocket-book, note-book, or memo tablet ? These little combinations of writing materials are now very generally used, and their popularity is best attested by the wonderful varieties of design, shape, and materials brought to bear upon their manufacture. Some pocket-books are made of fancy leaves, ornamental edgings and beautiful paper, good leather backs, and elastic band or brass buckle. Others, again, are made of the cheapest possible material, common paper, plain edges, board backs, and a very plain fastening. Pocket-books, like every other article in stationery, are made to make a trade as well as satisfy the wants of the general public. In some cases, good backs of strong serviceable leather, and good clasps or fastener are provided, to hold a book of cheap paper ; the masters arguing that, as the paper becomes exhausted before the cover, economy is best served by a strong cover to last out several books. This is sound policy. A pocket-book ought to be flexible rather than stiff ; it fits the pocket better, lasts longer, is more ornamental, and is lighter in weight. Note-books are often provided with an interior pocket, to hold cards, or other small papers, and a pencil. In many instances, note-books are the medium for encouraging very bad pencils, of such dimensions and qualities that the purchaser may safely enquire whether the pencil was not considered a necessary evil. At any rate, the pencils in note and pocket-books can be vastly improved. Let manufacturers add another penny to the price, and provide a pencil that will, first of all, mark neatly, keep a point, if it can ever get one, and, lastly, that can be made without the white top coming off immediately the pencil is used.

Thére are many other little and useful articles which might be comprised under the first heading of this essay. The writer knows how difficult it is to compile an even professedly hasty compendium of the stationery trade, and how remarkably easy it is to find out omissions after the labour is over. He trusts, however, that the anxiety to fulfil a difficult duty, may excuse many unintentional sins of both commission and omission.

Before advancing to the next great division of our subject, there is a threshold or porchway between the two divisions, and entering this, we find ourselves in the presence of hundreds of articles intended for graphic purposes in the office and household, which are at once a combination of manugraphic and typographic stationery. To illustrate our meaning, let us take the following well-known and highly useful goods:—Diaries, memo tablets, calender tablets, account-books of certain kinds, legal forms, bill stamps, luggage labels, &c., &c.

Diaries, calendars, and such-like stationery are to assist us in fixing engagements and remind us to keep them. Combined with the writing-desk or pad, a diary is most useful—indeed necessary. Calendars are of various forms, and are intended to keep us well informed as to the date of the month. They can be paper, wood, or iron, or a combination of all three, according to the ingenuity of the manufacturer. The most common are either a combination of iron and paper or wood and paper. Some are made to suspend, some to stand. All these goods, just as with pocket-books, are made in every conceivable modification of style, but all with one object. We also have pocket iaries, which are useful in their way, but these come under our second heading more particularly.

Certain account-books are sold by stationers, not only ruled and printed with such matter as will help the book-keeper, but small books for the household, and known as tradesmen's account-books, are a large item with many stationers. These small books serve the purpose of keeping a check on the baker, butcher, grocer, and, be it also said, the washerwoman, who, even in her humble profession, is adjudged worthy of emulating the same practices as her superiors. These little books cover a large ground, but may be said to be more or less alike, except as to the colour of the binding cover. They differ in sizes, but as a rule the term tradesmen's account-books will explain all about them.

Many legal forms are necessary to the retail stationer. He must keep apprenticeship indenture forms, forms of will, receipt of· rent books, notices between landlord and tenant, various receipt forms, and legal forms generally.

Shipping forms are necessary, especially to retailers in seaport towns and large manufacturing districts. Such stationery as bills of lading, log books, cargo books, and all similar documentary details, will be found most useful.

Bill stamps, book-post wrappers, agreement forms and sale notes are useful in any stationer's shop; whilst luggage labels, "apartments" cards, and any other books that contain printed matter to save handwriting, will find more or less ready sale.

Large houses will find it necessary to keep all the above goods in stock, as they relate entirely to manugraphic stationery and the direct consumption of paper. A few words as to the selection of stock may be modestly submitted as a conclusion to this part of our subject.

In all cases the buyer should consider his customers, their position in life, the money they can afford—not what they would like—to give; the tastes of his clients and the quantity he is likely to sell. Too many buyers overlook the character of their trade. They are carried away in admiration of goods which are too expensive for their customers, however attractive they may be as window goods. Many people go into a shop to ask the price of an article, being fearful to order it. Such customers are the germs, however, of a trade, and are as the bites to an ardent fisherman. It is good policy to be able to dispel any fears of a high price by selecting such goods as are not too

expensive, but possess at the same time an expensive appearance. Good finish is requisite. An article may be pure gold
and yet have no attraction about it. The foreign goods are
most attractive in *ensemble*, but will scarcely bear close examination. Good things and well finished are the best to make a
trade.

Upon the other hand, avoid "shoddy" stock. Gorgeous
articles with flimsy body are a mistake. In paper this is
especially the case. Very bad paper in our days is sold by a
striking wrapper. It is better to have a nice, neat, plain wrapper
with good paper.

The main thing for the retailer to avoid is not to tempt his
customers with low-priced goods. In the present day manufacturers are all bent upon a downward course of policy. Not
content with making a cheap article, they wish to out-Herod
Herod, and make goods so low that their neighbours cannot
compete. However feasible such a way of doing business may
seem, it is not strictly fair trade. It is a strenuous effort to
create a monopoly. All monopolies are bad, and against the
principle of free trade in commerce. Were this eagerness a
sentiment of honour and a desire to excel, there would be some
reason for overlooking the endeavour to secure a big trade; but
it is the exact reverse. All houses that enjoy a comparative
monopoly, and that reap the profits of a large connection,
do so because their goods are unsurpassed for excellence.
In the bad times of our trade the well-known and long-
established firms have not changed their policy, nor have they
changed their customers. They produce the best goods only,
and secure thereby the healthiest and most reliable trade. They
do not pander to the low feelings which actuate a policy of
greediness at the expense of the character of their manufacturers. The public have never exhibited any signs that the
lowest-classed article is necessary; on the other hand, there has
been, through the press and other agencies, a general exposition
of regret at the falling-off in our manufactures. Now is the
time to resolve upon a better course—a more honourable, and
surely a more profitable one.

There is one more branch of the stationers' trade yet to consider, which shall be treated at short notice, and that is, card, and uses of card. Card is merely the union of several sheets of paper. For this purpose two good writing papers are pasted together, and rolled until a fine surface is obtained. Sometimes three or more sheets are joined in the same way. The product is known as card. In the higher qualities, or ivory card—so-called from the smooth and white surface—the chief use is for visiting cards, invitations, and other similar complimentary purposes. The lower qualities of card frequently contain a middle—that is, a middle sheet, upon the two sides of which are pasted the outer surface paper. These middles may be commoner papers or board, either of wood or straw. In box-making, board is used. For printers' cards, such as " commercial," " printers'," &c., &c., a middle of common white paper is used. The surface-coloured cards are manufactured largely in Germany, and also in this country. They are made so that the outer surface shall be any tint or colour, according to order. Card is most exclusively used for advertising purposes, and for a business announcement also. Of late, during the past three years, the Americans have introduced cards with bevelled gold edges, a very handsome novelty, and especially well suited for many purposes ordinary card is used for. The ordinary cards are fanned out and bevelled by an emery wheel. Good quality of card is essential, so that expensive cards must always be the result of this process.

In passing to Typographic Stationery, we must regard a combination of typography and paper in two lights. We have first a plain combination, and we may, for mere example's sake, denominate books to represent this class. It would be folly to write much about books in an essay such as this. Books are not stationery, and would require a lecture all to themselves.

But the second division or luxurious combination demands some attention. There are certain *articles-de-luxe*, such as menu cards, ball programmes, and similar complimentary adjuncts which may be called stationery. These goods, mostly, if not entirely, of Parisian origin, are a new branch of business which stationers are pushing vigorously. Complimentary stationery, such as Christmas cards, Easter, New Year, Birthday and other similar cards are much of the same character, viz.: typographic stationery. Christmas cards and other like cards are a very nice exposition of kindly feeling at certain season-able times, and we all know the pleasant sentiments connected with a seasonable greeting. It is a happy form of business which can soothe and charm the cares and situations of social life. Never did the papermaker and printer unite for a more worthy object than the spread of good-will and good-wishes among humanity. The Christmas card, and we take it as a type, is an emblem of friendship and love, and is a design so gentle and pretty in itself, that it is fit only to be represented with a relative amount of artistic feeling. The introduction of Christmas cards took place just twenty years ago. At that time the pre-sent head of a large and esteemed firm of stationers was paying a visit on the Continent, and he happened to catch a sight of a pretty little card in a shop window, in the street of one of the German watering places. The card was very simple, contain-ing a small floral design and some kind words. Its sympathetic character, and further, its attractive appearance, impressed the practical Englishman, who bought the card, and with the assis-tance of experiment and ideas thoroughly excited by inspiration, developed this little card into what is now a gigantic business. The first cards were printed in Berlin, Germany being then the only country for high-class lithography. Afterwards in a town in the north of England, the first Christmas card was devised, and sold to the public for two-pence.

As in menu and other coloured cards, Christmas cards are an embodiment of culture, taste and typographic skill. Our firms can now accomplish everything, so far as colour printing is concerned, but the design is what in many cases rules the public. Generally the average public like floral groups. They are always pretty, but sometimes grossly inapplicable to the purpose. For instance, Christmas cards are really groups of summer flowers and the most delicate offspring of the warm weather. Why should they be a Christmas greeting? Are our artists obliged to seek their designs in summer flowers? are our artists unable to collect from all the wondrous beauties of wintry scenery and vegetation the wherewithal to exhibit their intent? Surely not. Buyers of Christmas and other cards argue, that whatever sells and makes a trade, that must be our line, and buyers are right after all. But there is a power in man to lead, though he may not be able to drive. Let the trade lead the public to the highest and most consistent pinnacle of art, whence they will view a picture that shall be more charming, because it will gratify all senses, and combine with what is pleasing to the sight, that which is in consonance with the mind.

The next item for a stationer to consider is playing-cards. These cards are so old and so well-known that any lengthy remarks need not be given. At the same time, they possess so many points of interest, and take so prominent a position in the domestic life of every civilized country, that a whole book would not exhaust the topic. Many silly people connect playing-cards with a gentleman who, it is said, " is not so black as he is painted." Narrow-minded people must always exist. The world would not possibly go round if everybody were to turn of the same mind. On our part, whilst deprecating gambling in every possible form, as an abuse of a pastime thoroughly innocent, we cannot but think that playing-cards help to amuse and instruct. A game at whist is, perhaps, less provocative of mischief than a tea-meeting, and requires certainly much more temperate behaviour on the part of all concerned. Many persons, who have a horror of horse-racing, do not object to ride in a cab; on the same ground, it is possible to play a game at cards "for love," and run no risk of future misery. We make these remarks on behalf of the manufacturers of playing-cards, whose grateful acknowledgments we accept in anticipation.

The trade nomenclature has of late years undergone considerable extension. Formerly, all good cards were called "moguls." Then, as other qualities came in, we had 1st, 2nd, 3rd, 4th, 5th moguls, and so on, thereby producing much confusion. Now, however, the old-fashioned title of moguls has extended to Harrys, Club Harrys, Highlanders, Andrews,

Harlequins, Pantaloons, Statesmen, Rajahs, Viceroys, &c., &c., and it is likely that the convenience which has been found to result from the adoption of distinctive titles for certain grades of cards, will lead to further amplification. Now, a buyer can specify Harrys or Pantaloons, knowing that each title has a certain standard of quality and price.

The manufacture of playing-cards is one of considerable intricacy, involving very careful manipulation, skill, and careful application of manufacturing process to and in all the materials used.

Whatever be the grade or quality of the playing-cards made, the same amount of care is required in both the card and the printing. The processes of making a playing-card from the raw material to the stage in which it reaches the public are multifarious, and the last is as important as the first. Any failure in any process, no matter how perfectly all previous processes have been accomplished, will render the entire work valueless. People buying cards should remember this, and not grumble at having to give good prices.

The card is composed of two or several sheets of paper properly joined, and the card thus formed is enamelled on one or both sides, after which it receives the decorative printing. Common cards are always sold by the gross, and the more expensive by the dozen. Some old games have been resuscitated of late, such as Quadrille, Poker (the old game of Brag), and others ; these, with Napoleon, have packs specially prepared, and are sold under distinctive names. The two general games are whist and bezique, for which the ordinary packs of 52 cards are in most request. The use of playing-cards has been alluded to already. Calendars, diaries—large and pocket, certain kinds of show cards, and a thousand and one other varieties of typographical stationery might be mentioned ; but their very existence and manipulation are so dependent upon the printer, that it will be advisable to omit any details about them.

All other combinations of card and colour printing may be said to be printers' work, and we may therefore think our task about finished. It has been an arduous, but a pleasant one. Arduous—on account of its great proportions, and from an anxiety to do it with all might and strength. Pleasant—because it has brought the writer in contact with many kind friends, to whom he owes more than he can express. This article has afforded one more opportunity for the experience of such kind assistance as would grace a life-long friendship rather than a pleasant business connection. To the gentlemen who have informed me on many points, let me tender my sincere thanks, and whatever merit there may be in this fractional effort to do justice to a great subject, all appreciation is due to their kind and valuable assistance.

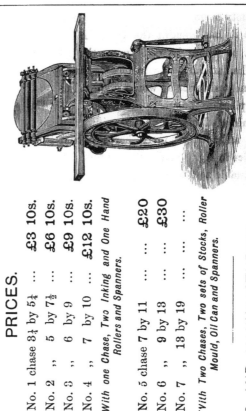
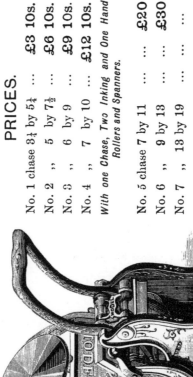

CATALOGUE.

THE DESCRIPTIONS OF THE EXHIBITS
HAVE BEEN SUPPLIED BY THE EXHIBITORS.

SPECIAL POSITIONS,
CENTRE OF GREAT HALL.

CHAPIN, J. L. & Co., 46, Rathbone Place, London, W.

Platen Printing Machine. " Gally's Patent Improved Universal," built for the Inventor (Merritt Gally) by the Colts' Arms Manufacturing Co., Hartford, U.S.A.

" Gem " Paper Cutting Machine (G. H. Sanboni's Patent), built by the Standard Machinery Co., Mystic River, Connecticut, U.S.A.

General Printers' Novelties :—Mason's Patent Adjustable Book Support. Lowell's Steel-plate Menu and Programme Engraved Cards.

" *American Model Printer*." Published by Kelly & Bartholomew, N.Y.

" Elm City " Card Cutter (patented), manufactured by H. P. Hubbard, New Haven, Connecticut, U.S.A.

"Little Giant," Rule and Lead Cutter, manufactured by Golding & Co., Boston, U.S.

Vanderburgh, Wills & Co.'s Wood Type and "Eagle" Printer's Cabinet.

Megill's Patent Adjustable Steel Gauge Pins and Feed Guides.

American Fancy Type. Case of Type and Specimen Books of Mackellar, Smith & Jordan, Philadelphia, Farmer, Little & Co., New York, Cincinatti Type Foundry, James Connor & Sons, New York, Boston Type Foundry, and others.

PERRY & Co., LIMITED, 18, 19 & 20, Holborn Viaduct, London, E.C. Works, 36, Lancaster Street, Birmingham.

Steel Pens, Pencils, Penholders, Paper Binders, Pencil Cases, Elastic Bands, Stationers' Sundries, Stationers' Cabinet Ware & Pocket Cutlery, American Clocks, Toys, and other novelties.

SQUINTANI, C. G. & Co., 3, Ludgate Circus Buildings, London, E.C.

The "Model" Printing Press for hand, foot, and steam power.

Paper Cutting and Perforating Machines.

Engine and Boiler combined (Outridge's Patent).

New Patented Locking-up Apparatus, "Twin Quoins" (Squintani's Patent).

Registered Gauge Pins, Rotary Mitreing Machine, "Little Giant" Rule and Lead Cutter, and several other new articles for Stationers, Printers and Bookbinders.

STACY, D. S., 62, Upper Street, London, N.

Specimens of Photography, taken by D. S. Stacy.

Stationery and Fancy Goods, &c.

Relievo in Plaster (subject "The Heathen Chinee." Bret Harte). Exhibited by Miss Billows, 19, Lyme St., N.W.

Statuette (subject "The Little Match Girl.")   ,,

Andersen's Fairy Tales (photographs of the same). ,,

BAYS ON GROUND FLOOR.

Nos. 1 to 24.

1. HAZELL, WATSON & VINEY, 6, Kirby Street, Hatton Garden, London, E.C.

Diamond Self-Clamp Cutting Machine.

KENDELL, THOMAS, Engineer, 26, Norfolk Place, Shoreditch, London, E.

Lever Cutting Machine for cutting Envelopes out of Flat Paper.

Folding Machine for Folding, Gumming and Stamping when cut.

Stamping Press for stamping Relief, Cameo, or Plain.

Gumming Machine for gumming Top Flaps of Envelopes.

Cutters for cutting the Flat Paper under Lever Machine.

2. EVERLING, H., 26, Rue Cadet, Paris.

Agent: C. PAETOW, 8, Old Jewry, London, E.C.

Brissard Patent Two-Cylinder Ruling Machine. This Machine rules from 4,000 to 6,000 sheets per hour on both sides simultaneously, and in two or three colors. Only one person is necessary to attend to the machine, which can be worked by hand or insignificant steam-power. It feeds and delivers the sheets automatically without the assistance of guides, and with great regularity. One intelligent person, even unaccustomed to ruling, can superintend several of these machines at one time.

Brissard Patent One-Cylinder Ruling Machine. This Machine is exactly the same as above, only ruling one side of the sheet at a time.

Horack Dasymeter, or Instrument to measure resistance of paper and its elasticity, 30 m/m long, 40 m/m wide, and 120 m/m high.

Three-Side Cutting Machine, for trimming post, note and writing paper on three sides without stoppage. This Machine is in use at the Mills of Messrs. Alexander Pirie & Sons, of Aberdeen, who have expressed to us their extreme satisfaction with its working.

Lhermitte's Improved Perforating Machine, for interrupted and uninterrupted Perforation. By simple turning of the pegs any interrupted perforation in the sheet can be obtained. The pegs, whether they work or not, are always guided, and can neither bend nor break.

Lhermitte's Improved Circular Board Cutter and Tracer, for Box-making. This Machine cuts boards to whatever size desired, and scratches them at the same time for folding the boards for box-making purposes. The same can also simply serve for the cutting of boards, cards, tickets, &c.

Papier Ambré. This Cigarette Paper is solidified at one end with melted amber, and thus avoids sticking to the lips, nor does it allow the nicotine to get into the mouth.

3. HEIM, W. F., Offenbach-on-Maine.

London Agent: L. TIDÉN, 11, Queen Victoria Street, London, E.C.

Paper Calendar.

Three Paper Cutting Machines.

4. SALMON, JAMES, 12, Parsonage, Manchester.

Mark Smith's Patent Flyer or Demy Reliance Printing Machine.

" Victory " Guillotine Cutting Machine.

Salmon's Eclipse Guillotine Cutting Machine.

Salmon & Co.'s Patent Bronzing Machine.

Salmon & Co.'s Patent Stone Grinding Machine.

Salmon & Co.'s Patent Scoring Machine.

Salmon & Co.'s Patent Perforating Machine.

5. CATTELL, A. S. & Co., 17 and 18, Bear Alley, London, E.C.

> Cattell's Process of producing Relief Blocks for Letter Press Printing called Zinco-Typography (working), with Specimens and Electrotypes taken from said blocks. (See Advertisement, p. 223.)

6. WEBSTER, G. E. & Co., Central Chambers, Market Street, Nottingham.

> Webster's Duplex Patent System of Gas Lighting, Globes, Photometers, Pressure Gauges, Governors.
> Webster & Fisher's Low Pressure Argands.
> Fancy Articles in Bronze.
> Figures, &c.

PROCTOR & WALLIS, Talbot Engine Works, Tustin Street, London, S.E.

> Edwards' New Patent Improved "Gas Engine," 2-man power.
> Edwards' New Patent Improved "Gas Engine," 2-horse power.
> 2-horse power Talbot Combined Steam Engine and Boiler.
> An assortment of New Patent Wrought Iron "Gap" Pulleys for attaching to Shafting without interfering with the rest of the machinery.

*** The Right Hon. E. DWYER GREY, M.P., Lord Mayor of Dublin.

> First volume *Freeman's Journal* dated 1763.
> Copies of current numbers *Freeman's Journal, Weekly Freeman, Dublin Evening Telegraph,* and *Irish Lance.*

7. NOTTING, W., Enterprise Works, Bowling Green Lane, Farringdon Road, London, E.C.

> Alexandria Hand-Printing Press.
> Improved " Columbian " Press.

Improved Lever and Roller Galley Proof Presses.

Specimens of Brass Rule and Ornamental Designs in ditto.

Printers' Sundries, &c.

8. DAY & COLLINS, 50 and 52, Fann Street, London, E.C.

Wood Engraving, Wood Letter Bulks, Facia Letters, Cases, Composing Frames, Case Racks, Forme Racks, Galley and Letter Board Racks, Imposing Surfaces, Wetting Troughs, Reglet and Furniture, Composing Sticks, Mallets, Planers, &c.

9. WOLFF, E. & SON, 55, Great Queen Street, Holborn, W.C., and Falcon Pencil Works, Battersea, London, S.W.

A few of the processes illustrating the manufacture of Black Lead Pencils by Steam Machinery, viz., Sawing the cedar into sticks, Grooving the cedar for reception of Black Lead, Inserting the Black Lead into cedar casing, Rounding the Pencils; the manufacture of Ball Programme Pencils on an improved principle.

Samples of Black Lead, or Graphite, in various stages of manufacture. (See also page 198, for stand of other articles.)

10. BIRMINGHAM MACHINISTS' Co., The, Great Queen Street Works, Birmingham.

"Invictus" Platen Printing Machine of entirely new construction. Improved Inking and Throw-off Movements.

Improved Stereotype Apparatus.

Patent "Simplissimus" Self-Inking Hand Press.

IHLEE & HORNE, 31, Aldermanbury, London, E.C.

Specimens of Sala's Wood for Binding purposes; also specimens of Binding in Leatherette and Feltine, &c

11. IHLEE & HORNE, 31, Aldermanbury, London, E.C.

> Patent Bookfolding Machine, by F. Martini & Co., Rifle Manufacturers.
>
> Patent Bookfolding and Sewing Combination Machine.
>
> Colonel De La Sala's Patent Pliable Wood for covering books.
>
> Patent Leatherette for book covering.
>
> Feltine, a substitute for Bookbinders' Cloth.
>
> Patent Pandograph, a Machine for Enlarging and Reducing Drawings.

12. MIDDLETON, T. & Co., Loman Street, Southwark, London, S.E.

> "Bacon's" Patent Multiple Color Printing Apparatus, by Messrs. T. Middleton & Co., fitted to a Double Demy HARRILD & SONS' Registered Bremner Machine.

BOND, WILLIAM HENRY, 25, Richmond Street, Old Street, London, E.C.

> The Ashley Paper Feeder (Waldo's Patent) or Mechanical Layer-on (W. H. Bond, sole proprietor and manufacturer.) This machine is an attachment for Letter-press, Litho', Perforating and the like Paper Printing or Stamping Machines requiring to be fed with sheets of paper or of card, one sheet at a time. It lays on perfectly and equally well all descriptions of paper, thick or thin, wet or dry. It dispenses with points entirely. The Feeder can be quickly adjusted to feed any size of sheet, from that of the full capacity of the feed-board to that of a note sheet, and in all grades, with equal exactness. For color printing it is unequalled for its precision and uniformity, combined with the speed of its register, and for this class of work it is specially advantageous for the printer.

13. LAWRENCE BROS., Viaduct Works, Farringdon Road, London, E.C.

Undercut Self-Clamping Cutting Machines (patented) for hand or power.

Quire-folding Machines for Paper Mills, Account Book Makers, &c.

Rotary Perforating Machines.

14. CROSLAND, WILLIAM, New Street, Miles Platting, Manchester.

The "Advance" Paper Cutting Machine (Crosland's patent.)

Rotary Scoring Machine.

Crosland's Patent Combined Cutting and Scoring Machine.

Rotary Millboard Cutting Machine.

Corner Cutting Machine.

Crosland's Patent Luggage Label Folding Machine.

Patent Litho' Stone Grinding and Polishing Machine, &c.

15–16. TIDCOMBE, G., & SON, Paper Makers' Engineers, Watford, Herts.

Ibotson's Patent Strainer with noiseless action.

Strainer Plates of copper and brass.

A Patent Pulp Refiner.

Holloway's Patent Apparatus for working the Paper-making Machine without stopping.

A singles heet Paper-cutting Machine for cutting watermarked papers with Pitts' Patent Sheet-collecting Apparatus.

HOLLINGWORTH, Messrs., Turkey Mill, Maidstone.

Paper.

17. Newsum, Wood & Dyson, Meadow Road Printing Machine Works, Leeds.

Improved Double Double Crown Litho' Machine for chromo and fine color printing.

Crown Litho' Machine fitted with Newsum's Patent Taking-off Apparatus; also adapted for Letter-press.

18. Andrew, J. E. H., Waterloo Road, Stockport. *London Depot:* Castle Works, Castle Street, Kingsland. N.

Two-man-power ($\frac{1}{4}$ H.P.) Bisschop Patent Gas Engine price £35, driving a Demy Harrild & Sons' Registered, Bremner Machine, with Stopping Cylinder, and the new Self-acting Cylindrical Sheet Flyers.

Two-man-power ($\frac{1}{4}$ H.P.) Bisschop Patent Gas Engine, price £35, driving a Crown Folio Harrild & Sons' new Patent Treadle " Bremner " Platen Machine.

Two-man-power ($\frac{1}{4}$ H.P.) Bisschop Patent Gas Engine price £35, driving Patent Quire-folding Machine by Richmond & Co.

19. Brehmer, Aug., 19, Cow Cross Street, London, E.C.

Brehmer's Patent Wire Sewing and Stitching Machines for Account Books, Novels, School Books, Bibles, Music Books, Catalogues, Circulars, Pamphlets, &c.

Brehmer's Patent Machine for Rounding the Backs of Account Books and Printed Books.

Peck, Robt., 90, Bartholomew Close, London, E.C.

Specimens of Cloth Binding and Wire Sewing.

20. RIDDLE & COUCHMAN, 22, Southwark Bridge Road, London, S.E.

Specimens, viz., " You dirty boy" Show-bill. Show-bill of Pear's Soap Washing the Nigger White, 8ft. by 4ft. Show-bill of Powell's Balsam of Aniseed. Show-bill of Brook's Kitchen Crystal Soap.

Beautiful Floral Borders, Royal Sheets.

Chromo-Lithographs: " Cottage Home," " No More, Bobby," " Birds of the Months," &c., &c.

Borders for Certificates, Mottoes, Texts, and Business Purposes.

Illustrated Catalogues, Packets of Publishers' Cards, &c.

Lithographic Machine, by Deardin & Newsum, in full work, with Chromo-Lithographs.

21. ULLMER, F., Standard Works, Cross Street, Farringdon Road, London, E.C.

Demy Standard Printing Machine.

Crown Albion Printing Press.

26-in. powerful Guillotine Paper Cutting Machine.

27-in. Perforating Machine.

Mitreing, Eyelet, and Paging Machines.

Card Cutter.

Imposing Surface and Frame.

Improved Folding Case Rack.

Frame with Rack and 9 Half Cases.

Galleys, Cases, Wrought Iron Chases, Treadle Stabbing Machine, and Printers' Materials and Sundries.

Demy Improved Standard Printing Machine fitted with Flyer.

22. BRADBURY, WILKINSON & Co., Farringdon Road, London, E.C.

> Cylinder Plate Printing Machine in motion (shown for the first time), performing the whole operation of inking, wiping, and printing copper or steel plates.

23. CROSSLEY BROS., 116, Queen Victoria Street, London, E.C.

> Half-horse " Otto " Silent Gas Engine.

INGLE, H. & Co., 102, Shoe Lane, London, E.C.

> Improved Patent City Printing Machine, double-crown size, with flyers. Speciality—lightness in running and ease in making ready.

FAIRHOLME & Co., 9, Great Winchester Street, E.C.

> The " Acme " Composition for Clothing Printers' Rollers.
>
> The Multiscript and Hektograph Copying Apparatus.
>
> POWELL'S Quadrant Demy Machine.

24. TURNBULL, JOHN, Jun., 184, Buchanan Street, Glasgow.

> Two Patent Frictionless Steam Engines, fitted with the " Simple " Cut-off Valve Gear and " Perfect " Piston Packing. Having parallel motion at both ends, which, causing the Piston to float, and dispensing with Guide and Guide Blocks, the friction, tear and wear, and consumption of lubricants are in a remarkable degree reduced. The utmost speed may be attained, and the Engine may be run either way with equal ease. All

the parts are accessible, strong, and substantial, and highly finished throughout. One is a Single Cylinder Non-condensing Engine, 12-in. diameter, 2-ft. stroke; the other a Compound Tandem Engine, having Cylinders 15-in. and 9-in. diameter respectively, both 2-ft. stroke. Either of these Engines will develope 40 horse-power with 60-lbs. of steam.

GROUND FLOOR.—EAST SIDE.

OFFICIAL CATALOGUE OFFICE.

25. FENNER & APPLETON, 77, St. John Street, London, E.C.

The Lightning Printing Machine (Croxon's).

Double Ruling Machine (Shaw's).

Single Striker Ruling Machine (Shaw's).

Envelope Cutting Machine (Fenner's).

Envelope Folding Machine (Fenner's).

Account Books and Envelopes.

26. FURNIVAL & Co., 7, Charterhouse Street, Holborn Circus, London, E.C., and Ogden Street, Ardwick, Manchester.

Patent "Express" Lithographic Printing Machine, Demy size, fitted with Hird's Patent Pneumatic Deliverer, and also with a new and greatly improved system for Diagonal Inking and Distributing.

Gill's Patent Hot Rolling Machine, Rolls 26 inches long, for drying and pressing sheets direct from the Printing Machine, giving a very superior finish to the same.

32-inch Patent " Express " Self Clamp Guillotine. By a foot lever, the platen is brought down on to the work for the purpose of adjustment. The Machine is started, clamps, cuts and returns in 3 seconds. A 32-inch machine will cut 800 gross of copy-books in a week of 55 hours.

26-inch Patent " Express " Hand Guillotine, with Planed Iron Tables, and fitted with all the latest improvements.

12-inch Patent " Universal " Job and Label Diagonal Cutting Machine.

Foolscap Folio Patent " Caxton " Platen Printing Machine, with greatly increased inking power, Patent self locking chase bed, throw-off motion, &c. &c.

27. HOPKINSON & COPE, Farringdon Road, London, E.C.

The Genuine " Albion " Press, invented by R. W. Cope, and improved by Hopkinson.

The " Universal " Treadle Platen Machine.

The Payne's Patent Demy Color Wharfedale Machine, with double rolling and extra distribution and flyers.

The H. S. Demy Treadle Wharfedale Machine, with flyers.

28. MASSON & SCOTT, Engineers and Millwrights, York Place, York Road, Battersea, London.

Measuring Machine for measuring Caustic Liquors and other Liquids.

Finished Chilled Calender Roll, English iron.

Samples of Straw Pulp, &c., made by improved process.

29. ANNANDALE, ALEXANDER, Beltonford Paper Works, Dunbar, N.B.

Patent Damping Machine for Damping Paper in the Web, preparatory to glazing or printing.

Worn Knotterbottoms, reclosed and renewed by patent process.

Sample Reams of the various qualities and descriptions of Paper produced at the Beltonford Paper Works.

GROUND FLOOR.—NORTH SIDE.

30. MANN, G. & Co., Paragon Works, Elland Road, Leeds.

Lithographic Printing Machine, in work, for Colour Printing.

31. GREENWOOD & BATLEY, Albion Works, Leeds.

Three-and-a-half horse-power Brown's Patent Caloric Engine.

Greenwood & Kritch's Patent " Sun " Platen Printing Machine. Can be worked by treadle or power.

31A. RODDICKS, ALFRED, 311, New North Road, Islington, London, N.

Sample of Stereo Plate, as used by the *Standard*, *Telegraph*, *Daily News*, and most of the principal Newspaper Printers in England and America.

OFFICIAL CATALOGUE OFFICE.

31B. TURNBULL, C. E. & Co., 5, Charterhouse Buildings, London, E.C.

The " Utility Inkstand," registered February 21st, 1877, No. 5902.

The " Utility Winged Tray Work Box," registered April 5th, 1879, No. 6159.

The " Utility Despatch and Writing Case," registered April 26th, 1878, No. 6030.

32. BERTRAM, GEORGE & WILLIAM, St. Katherine's Works, Sciennes, Edinburgh.

Paper Cutting Machine, with slitting and revolving cross cut'knives, to cut from several reels as required.

Strainer of Knotter Plates, as used for all classes of paper.

33. CLOWES, WILLIAM & GEORGE, Stamford Street, London, S.E.

William & George Clowes' " Hooker's " Patent Type Composing Machine.

William & George Clowes' Electrotype Black-leading Machine.

34. WATERLOW & SONS, LIMITED, London Wall, Great Winchester Street, Finsbury Works, and Parliament Street, London.

Waterlow's Patent Improved Autographic Press. A portable machine for printing from stone, by means of which every person may become his own printer.

The Stylographic Pen.

Waterlow & Sons' Patent Railway Ticket Printing Machine ; Ticket Counting Machine ; Ticket Destroying

Machine; Ticket Long Shearing Machine; Ticket Chopping Machine; Ticket Tying-up Machine; Ticket Issue Cases; Ticket Dating Presses; Ticket Nippers; and Type Numbering Machines.

Waterlow & Sons' Morse, Wheatstone, and other Telegraph Paper.

35. LONG, THOMAS & Co., Engineers and Machine Makers, 26, S. B. Canongate, Edinburgh.

Double Demy Letterpress "Wharfedale" Machine, with moulds, pointing apparatus, and flyer complete.

36. FIELDHOUSE & ELLIOT, Otley, Yorkshire.
London Agents: HESTER & SON, 7, Bride Court, Ludgate Circus.

"Reliance" Wharfedale Printing Machine, fitted with flyers for self-delivery.

29-inch Millboard Cutting Machine.

Bookbinder's Nipping Press, 14-inch by 12-inch.

16-inch Card Cutting Machine.

Roller Moulds, &c.

37. BERTRAM, JAMES & SON, Engineers, Leith Walk Foundry, Edinburgh.

Knotter or Strainer designed to take the place of the ordinary Flat Jog Knotter, consisting of a set of machine-cut brass plates which are fixed in the vat and remain stationary. The action is caused by the simple application of an air-pump, which keeps in constant motion an india-rubber disc or flap below the plates, thus causing a perfect action. The Pump can be made to work two or more of these Knotters, and is also applied to Revolving Knotters.

Machine designed for the purpose of crushing Soda Ash to any degree of smallness, thus saving much time and steam in the dissolving pans. It consists of one fixed and one moveable corrugated jaw, between which the large pieces of Soda Ash are placed. The moveable jaw is driven by a simple arrangement of eccentric spur wheel and pinion. This Machine can crush 12 to 14 cwt. of Ash in ten hours.

38. M'CORMICK & BEGG, 170, Buchanan Street, Glasgow.

Jones' Patent Process and Patent Improved Dry Pressing Machine. By this process, and with this machine, printed and folded sheets are perfectly pressed without set-off, and without fuller or glazed boards being interposed between them.

Hickok's Improved Patent No. 0. A. Pennsylvanian Ruling Machine, with Patent Striker, which rules any number of Stops as easily as print lining.

GROUND FLOOR.—WEST SIDE.

38A. ZAPP & BENNETT, Steam Printers and Lithographers to the Trade, 52A, Bow Lane, Cheapside, London, E.C.

Lithographed "Perambulator Bill" in 5 colours, printed at five workings on a whole sheet of quadruple double crown paper. Size 60in. by 40in.

Lithographed "Bicycle Bill" in 3 colours, printed at three workings, on a whole sheet of quadruple crown paper. Size 40in. by 30 in.

Lithographed " Court Lance Bill " in 6 colours, printed at six workings, on a whole sheet of quadruple crown paper. Size 40in. by 30in.

Lithographed "Cigarette Bill " in 2 colours, printed at four workings, on two sheets of quadruple demy paper. Size 70in. by 45in.

38AA. ELLISSEN & Co., 10, Type Street, Finsbury, London, E.C.

Portrait of H.R.H. the Princess of Wales ; Portrait of the Right Honourable the Earl of Beaconsfield, K.G.

38B. REED, SIR C. & SONS, Fann Street Letter Foundry, London, E.C.

The new French "Speciale" Roller Composition, lately introduced into this country, is made with a special view of combining durability with efficiency. It is less liable to shrink, and requires far less washing than most compositions. It has been found to stand all temperatures, and to work equally well for slow fine-art or rapid news work. *See testimonials, &c., accompanying exhibit.*

38c. WILLIAMS, R. H. & SONS, South Bermondsey Railway Station, London, S.E.

Bright Turned Shafting.
Pulleys, Gearing, Leather Belting.
Steam Boilers.
,,　　Donkey Pumps.
,,　　Engine and Boiler Combined.

39. MARSHALL, SONS & Co., LIMITED, Brittania Works, Gainsborough, and 3, King Street, Cheapside, London, E.C.

12-horse Improved Horizontal Fixed Steam Engine, (Class C) fitted with Patent Automatic Expansions Valve Gear. Price £158.

6-horse Improved Horizontal Fixed Steam Engine (Class B) fitted with Patent Automatic Expansions Valve Gear. Price £89.

4-horse Improved Stationary Steam Engine, in Locomotive Multitubular Boiler. Price £140.

1½-horse Vertical Steam Engine, with independent Boiler, complete. Price £60.

3-horse Vertical Steam Engine without Boiler, but with Tank, Base, and Force Pump. Price £40.

The whole of the above are manufactured by Exhibitors.

GROUND FLOOR.—SOUTH SIDE.

40. BEVIS, HENRY, Banner Manufacturer, 140, Pentonville Road, London, N.

Specimen Banners used for Decorations of Ball Rooms, Schools, Fêtes, &c., and Samples of Signs for Advertising Purposes.

40A. HUMPHREYS, J. C., 45, Borough Road Station, London, S.E., and Knightsbridge.

Portable Iron House, specially constructed for printers and lithographers.

Studio in Iron, for photographers.

Galvanized Iron Roofing.

Felt for printing purposes.

ROW NO. 25.

41. COLLINS, WM., SONS, & Co., LIMITED, Bridewell
    Place, New Bridge Street, London, E.C.

> Writing-papers, Envelopes, Boxes of Stationery, Pape-
> teries, &c.
>
> Account-books, Memorandum-books, Letter-books, Ex-
> ercise-books, Head-line Copy-books Drawing-books.
>
> Sundries : Leather Goods, Writing-desks, Secretaires,
> Purses, Pocket-books, Tourist Dispatch-cases, Slates,
> Christmas and New Year Cards, Mathematical Instru-
> ments, Colour-boxes, &c.

42. BADDELEY & REYNOLDS, Die-Sinkers, 19 and 20,
    Old Bailey, E.C.

> Lever and Screw Embossing Presses, Perforating
> Presses, Numerators, Endorsing Presses, "Paragon"
> Dating Stamps, India-rubber Stamps, Endorsing
> Inks, "Paragon" Copyograph, Die-sinking in pro-
> cess, Medals, Relief Stamping and Illuminating.

43. PAETOW, C., 8, Old Jewry, London, E.C.
    Agent for EXHIBITORS in Bay No. 2 and Nos. 44
    to 48 in Row 25.

44. WAERN, C. F. & Co., Gothenburg, Sweden.

> Wood Pulps in their various stages, and Wood Middles,
> manufactured at Langed Mill, Forswick Mill, Töcksfors
> Mill, Spanga Mill, Carlsfors Mill, and Jössefors Mill.
> Also Chemically Prepared Wood Pulp, in various stages,
> manufactured by Backhammar Mill. Agent, C. Paetow,
> 8, Old Jewry, London, E.C.

45. JACOBSON, J. & Co., Hanover, Germany.

German Linen and Cotton Rags, a complete assortment of. Agent, C. Paetow, 8, Old Jewry, London, E.C.

46. GRELLINGEN WOOD PULP COMPANY, near Basel, Switzerland.

Aspen and Bleached Pine Pulps in their various stages. Agent, C. Paetow, 8, Old Jewry, London, E.C.

47. SIOU, C. & Co., Lanmeuil près Larche (Carrize), France.

Straw Papers in various qualities. Agent, C. Paetow, 8, Old Jewry, London, E.C.

48. HENGGELER, HAINWERLE & Co., Landquart, Switzerland.

Coloured Paper of various qualities. Agent, C. Paetow, 8 Old Jewry, London, E.C.

49. WERTHEIM, A. & Co., Cassel, Germany.

Linen and Cotton Rags and Jute Baggings for Paper Makers (a complete assortment of.)

50. ANDRAE, OSCAR, Relliehausen, near Dassel, Hanover.

Chemically Pure Filter Paper.
Ordinary Filter Papers.
Hand-made Packing Paper and Boards.

51. SPIRO, IGNAZ & SÖHNE, Prague, Bohemia.

Printing Papers.
Waterproof Packing Papers.
Packing Papers.
Wood Pulp Paper.
Wood Pulp Boards.

52. KALLAB, FERD. VICT., Dyer and Chemist, Wiese, near Jaegerndorf, Silesia, Austria.

Patent Improvements in the Method of Recovering Indigo, which method is applicable for other purposes.

Filter Papers.

Chief matter:—Regaining of Indigo from Rags, Patented for England, Austria, Hungary, France, Belgium and Italy. Prize of Honour, Berlin, 1878, at the International Exhibition of Stationery wares.

Scoured Indigo Dyed Rags.

Rags Freed from Indigo.

Indigo Regained from Indigo Dyed Rags.

Tissues Dyed with Indigo Regained from Rags.

53. BUSBRIDGE, G. F. & Co., East Malling Mills, Kent, and the Kent Paper Warehouse, 22, Queen Street, London, E.C.

Busbridge's Improved Vat Paper (Registered), superior to the best hand-made papers for strength, erasing, uniformity and cheapness; also the original "Malling" Mill Papers, Tinted and Drawing Papers, together with Patent Account Book Papers.

Busbridge's Improved Vat Drawing Paper, specially manufactured for Artists and Draughtsmen.

54. MEAD, HENRY, 189 & 190, Bishopsgate Street Without, London.

General Manufactured Stationery and Account Books, Metallic, Pocket and Memorandum Books of every description, Fancy Goods, &c.

55. LANHAM ROLLER Co., The, LIMITED, 75, Fleet Street, London, E.C.

Typographic and Lithographic Printing Rollers; likewise showing the material of which they are composed in the various stages of manufacture.

56. ATKINSON, W. H., 156, Camberwell Road, London, S.E.

Samples of Vermilion.

57. COOKE, ALFRED, Leeds.

Picture Almanacks for all Trades.

ROW NO. 26.

FROM EAST END TO CENTRE.

58. COLLINS, WILLIAM, SONS & Co., LIMITED, Bridewell Place, New Bridge Street, London.

59. HOLLIDGE, E. J., 17, Wharf Road, City Road, London, N.

Writing and Copying Inks of every description, Black and Coloured.

Ink Powders.

" Graph " and Endorsing Inks.

Liquid Dyes, &c.

60. GOW, BUTTERFIELD & Co. (late Butterfield & Mason), Bowling Green Lane Buildings, Farringdon Road, London, E.C.

Reproductions in Chromo-Lithography of High-class Oil Paintings and Water Colour Drawings, with specimens of Show Cards, Trade Emblems, &c.

M

61. ENGLISH, J. & Co., 23, Budge Row, London, E.C.

Playing Cards, Printing Cards, Card-boards, Paste-boards, Mounting Boards, Perforated Boards.

62. AVALON LEATHER BOARD Co., The, Street, near Glastonbury. *Agents:* G. SMYTH & Co., 46, Cannon Street, London, E.C.

Fence Boards and Glazing Boards for Paper Makers.
Cards for Jacquard Looms.
Leather Board for Stiffeners and Inner Soles of Boots, and Shoes, and for Portmanteaus.
Waterproofed Leather Board.

63. MENDIP PAPER MILLS Co., LIMITED (No. 364), Wells, Somerset. *Agents:* G. SMYTH & Co., 46, Cannon Street, London, E.C.

Finest Printings and Writings, Plate and Lithographic Papers, both white and coloured.
Samples and prices on application.

64. MONCKTON, WALTER & Co., Basted Paper Works, near Sevenoaks, Kent.

Imitation Hand-made Writing and Account Book Papers.
Linear, Banks, and Drawing Papers.

65. LEUNIG, F. & Co., 68, Upper Thames Street, E.C.

Paper Scale for showing correctly at a glance the weight of a Ream of Paper, containing either 480, 500, or 516 sheets, by weighing a single sheet; scale from ½lb. to 80lbs.
Millboard Scale for showing correctly at a glance the weight of a full sheet of Millboard; scale ½oz. to 4lbs.
Pocket Paper Scale ditto.
Postal Letter Scale; scale from ¼oz. to 12oz., and 15 to 345 grammes.

66. DAVIDSON, C. & SONS, LIMITED, Paper Manufacturers, 80, Upper Thames Street, London, and at Aberdeen, N.B.

Papers, Wrapping Papers, and Glazed Papers of every description ; White Papers, Browns, Greys, Middles, Manillas.

Davidson's New Paper Felt.

Paper Bags of every description.

67. HOOD, W. C., St. George's Dye and Colour Works, Walburgh Street, Cable Street, London, E.

Aniline Dyes.

Aniline Cycloids for Inks, Dyes, and Water Colours.

Liquid Printing Ink.

Glue and Gelatine.

Ultramarine, Fine Colours, &c.

68. SMITH, JEREMIAH & Co., 42, Rathbone Place, Oxford Street, London.

New Shapes of Envelopes.

Illuminating, and Relief Stamping.

New Designs for Memory Cards.

Tracing Cloth and Tracing Paper.

69. WATSON, E., 54, Paddington Street, London, W

Specimens of Bookbinding.

70. SCREEN, *with the following Exhibits :*—

HODSON, J. S., Originator and Hon. Secretary to the Caxton Celebration Exhibition, 1877

Caxton Celebration, 1877.

The Four Hundredth Anniversary of the Introduction of Printing into England by William Caxton.

Rélics of the Caxton Exhibition.

Fac-simile reprint of Caxton's " Booke of the Chesse."

Caxton Memorial, 1847.

Life of Caxton, by William Blades (Second Edition), 1877.

Caxton Celebration Catalogue.

The Caxton Bible, 1877. " Wholly printed and bound in 12 hours."

History of the Caxton Bible, by Henry Stevens.

The Bibles in the Caxton Exhibition, by Henry Stevens.

Report of Caxton Celebration, 1877.

Memorial of the Exhibition, printed on an old wooden press on paper made in the Exhibition.

Tickets of the various Public Meetings held during the Celebration.

PRINTERS' PENSION, ALMSHOUSE, AND ORPHAN ASYLUM CORPORATION.

Drawing of the Almshouses at Wood Green, built 1849.

Photograph of the Wings built 1871.

Prospectus of the Corporation.

List of Pensioners, with amounts received by each, from 1827 to 1875.

OETZMANN & Co., 67 to 79, Hampstead Road, London, N.W.

An original copy of the first newspaper published in Cyprus, printed part in English and part in Greek, also a full-size Carbon Photograph of same.

TERRY, STONEMAN, & Co., 82, Hatton Garden, London, E.C.

A frame of specimens of Mourning Stationery, including the newest designs in Memorial Cards and patterns of the various issues of their Oxford Mourning Note Paper and Envelopes, of which Terry, Stoneman, & Co. are the Proprietors.

FRITH, F. & Co., Reigate, Surrey.

Frith's Photographs of English and Foreign Cathedrals, Abbeys, Castles, Landscapes, &c. Frith's series comprise altogether more than 10,000 different subjects.

TAYLOR, THOMAS, Printers' Auctioneer, 7, Portugal Street, Lincoln's Inn, London.

" Caxton examining the first Proof Sheet from his Printing Press in Westminster Abbey." Chromo-litho, in 10 colours, by Vincent Brooks, Day & Son, from the Original Picture by Wehnert. Copyright, Drawings, Stones, and Stock of 4,900 to be disposed of. Apply to Exhibitor.

" Shakespeare's Conceptions," formed of 197 scraps, from an old edition of Shakespeare, and containing upwards of 400 characters. Arranged by Henry Sinclair, comedian. Plain Litho' and Tint. Copyright and stones to be disposed of. Apply to Exhibitor.

Ditto, a transfer, with addition of Birthplace and Church, for Dedications, &c.

BACON, E. & SON, Wilfrid Works, Chalk Farm Road, Camden Town, N.W.

Specimens of Machinagraphy as used for the Prevention of Forgery of Bank Notes, Bonds, Shares, Cheques, Bills of Exchange, Trade Marks, Labels, &c.

For Copperplate, Lithographic, Letterpress or Ductor Printing.

FIELD & TUER, 50, Leadenhall Street, London, E.C.

An extensive assortment of specimens of Printing (chiefly Letter-press) from English, American, Colonial, and Foreign Printers, originally sent for criticism in the columns of the *Paper and Printing Trades' Journal.*

R. C. Mackay's new and improved Machine for all kinds of Gold Lettering from printers' type upon any material without the use of glaire.

71. FIELD & TUER, 50, Leadenhall Street, London, E.C.

The Paper and Printing Trades' Journal.
Typographical Curiosities.
Carbonic and Manifold Papers.
Japanese Papers.
Extra-thin Manilla Tissues.
Novel Papers, Publications, &c.

ROW NO. 27.

FROM EAST END TO CENTRE.

72. DICKINSON, JOHN & Co., 65, Old Bailey, London, E.C.

Superfine Printing Paper and News in Webs and Reams.
Printed Books, Plates, and Maps.
Envelopes, Cards, and Surface Coloured Papers.

73. GOODE BROS., Clerkenwell Green, London.

Christmas and Birthday Cards, Satchets, Valentines, Calendars, Prints for Transferring and Miscellaneous Fancy and other Stationery.

74. KNEPPERS, W., NEPHEW, b. Ruger, Vienna, Austria. *Sole Agents :* BECK & POLLITZER, 211, Upper Thames Street, London, E.C.

Gelatine Fancy Papers.
Satin and Muslin Papers.

FIEGET, ADOLPH, Dresden, Saxony. *Sole Agents :* BECK & POLLITZER, 211, Upper Thames Street, E.C.

Small Hands and Small Caps.
Closet and Curling Papers.

75. LEWY, GEBRÜDER, Berlin and Königsberg. *Agents :* BECK & POLLITZER, 211, Upper Thames Street, E.C.

Rags and Paper Makers' Materials.

76. BENRATH & FRANK, Gelbe Mühle, near Duren, Prussia. *Sole Agent :* BUCK, ANT. A., 59, Mark Lane, E.C.

Tracing and Drawing Paper.

76A. SCHRAMM, CHRISTOPH, Offenbach-on-Maine, Germany.

Printers, Copperplate-Printers and Lithographers' Inks, black and coloured.

77. BOTELBERGE, G. & Co., Melle, near Ghent, Belgium. *Agents :* ARNATI & HARRISON, 44, Eastcheap, London, E.C.

Ultramarines blue, violet, and red, specially prepared for paper-making and paper-staining. Gold Medal at Paris, 1878. Established 1843.

78. ROCHE GOONBARROW CHINA CLAY COMPANY, LIMITED, The, Roche, Cornwall.

China Clay prepared for paper-makers' purposes. A " Treatise on China Clay, and How to Use it."

79. HARDTMUTH, L. & C., 14, Holborn Viaduct, London.

Black Lead and Coloured Chalk Pencils.
School, Music, and Book-slates.
China Inkstands, Pen-wipers, &c.
Specialité : " Graphite Comprime" Pencils, and Artists' Chalks in 48 various colours.

80. WADE, JOSIAH, Crown Works, Hopwood Lane, Halifax.

The Anglo-American "Arab" Patent Platen Machine, (size Foolscap Folio) adapted for steam and treadle.

81. REES, HENRY & Co., LIMITED, 196, Westminster Bridge Road, London.

Printed Metal Tablets for advertising.
Metal Tiles, a cheap substitute for Encaustic Tiles.
Printed and Decorated Metal Sheets for all purposes.
Flower Boxes for Windows, Conservatories, &c.
Mantle Pieces, &c.

82. TUCK, RAPHAEL, 177, City Road, London.

Christmas and New Year Cards.
Relief Scraps and Portraits.
Chromo Portraits of Celebrities.
Oleographs and Chromos.
Picture Frames.

83. LADD, J. H. & Co., 116, Queen Victoria Street, London, E.C.

The Boomer Patent Press, replacing Hydraulics, and superseding the Screw; worked by a combination of four Levers acting on Toggle Joints, through which pass a right and left hand Screw, so that when the arms are reaching centre the power is accumulating with every turn of the Screw.

84. EYRE & SPOTTISWOODE, Her Majesty's Printers, Bible Warehouse, Great New Street, Fetter Lane, London, E.C.

Specimens of Binding and Printing.
Bibles, Prayer Books, Church Services, &c.
Leather Goods in every variety.

Specimens of Chromo-Lithographic Works : Christmas,
Birthday, New Year, and Reward Cards.

Mathematical Instruments.

Water Colours, Drawing Materials.

Stationery Sundries, including many registered Novelties, &c.

ROW NO. 28.

FROM EAST END TO CENTRE.

85. DICKINSON, JOHN & Co., 65, Old Bailey, London,
E.C.

86. GOODE BROTHERS, Seckforde Street, Clerkenwell
Green, London.

87. MORDAN, F. & Co., Albion Works, 326, City Road,
London, E.C.

> Writing, Copying, and Ruling Inks :—Black, Red, Blue,
> and Fancy Colours, also Perfumed. Marking Inks with-
> out preparation. City of London Marking Ink re-
> quires no heating.
>
> Endorsing Inks for India-rubber Stamps :—Ticket Inks.
> Multiple Inks for use with any of the new copying
> processes.
>
> Soluble Ink Powders :—Black, Red, and Blue, specially
> prepared for Shippers, saving freight of bottle, &c.
> The Red and Blue Inks made from these Powders may
> be used for machine ruling.
>
> Household Dyes.
>
> Special Exhibit of experiments, shewing the superiority
> of F. Mordan's Neutral Non-corrosive Ink over ordinary
> Blue-Black Ink. Chemical illustration.

A permanent Black Ink made instantly from two Colourless Liquids.

Samples of Nut Galls, Raw Materials, and Chemicals used in the manufacture of Writing Inks.

Office Gum, in bottles fitted with Cap and Brush, and for refilling.

Double Strength Gum, of uniform strength and excellence.

Household Glue, for mending China, Glass, &c.

Sealing Wax:—F. Mordan's guaranteed quality Letter Wax; Engravers' Wax in stick and plate; Druggists' and Pipe Makers' Wax; Parcel Wax; Wine and Bottling Wax; Governmental and Post Office Wax, as made for Her Majesty's Postmaster-General, the Egyptian, Australian, and other Colonial Post Offices.

Hard India Wax, specially prepared for hot climates.

Bank of England Wax, as made by F. Mordan and his predecessors, Boatwright, Brown & Co., since the year 1797.

Fancy Coloured Wax, and Bride Wax. Wax used by the Lord Chancellor for the Great Seal of England.

Samples of Shellac, Vermilion, and the various materials and chemicals used in the manufacture of Sealing Wax.

Gold Pens:—" Magnum Bonum," or Presentation Pens; Barrister, Oblique, Ladies', and ordinary Slip Pens.

Specimens, illustrating the manufacture of a Gold Pen from the pure gold to completion.

Stationery Cabinets, Inkstands, Purses, Cutlery, Crystal Glass Inkstands, Pencils Cases, Quill Pens, Wafers, &c. &c.

88. EVERETT, WILLIAM HENRY, 22, Bouverie Street, Fleet Street, London, E.C.

W. H. Everett's Provincial Newspaper Stall.

On Sale Daily:—*Manchester Examiner, Leeds Mercury, Sheffield Independent, Irish Times, The Scotsman, Liverpool Courier, Liverpool Post, Liverpool Mercury, Bristol Times*

and Mirror, Newcastle Chronicle, Newcastle Journal, also
the weekly editions. These and others, see list, a copy
of which can be had on application at the stall, are
on sale daily at Everett's London and Provincial Advertising and Newspaper Offices, 22, Bouverie Street,
Fleet Street, E.C.

89. Rowney, J., 58, City Road, London, E.C.

Writings and Printings, Browns and Drabs, Small
Hands, Surface Coloured, and Marble Papers.
Straw Boards lined and unlined.
Wood Pulp Boards lined and unlined.
Coloured Pulp Printings.
Middles and Millboards.

90. Davis, Joseph & Co., 6, Kennington Park Road, London, S.E.

Barometer Dials, Lithographic and Copper-plate Sun-
dials and Compasses. Specific Gravity Tests—Printed
Scales. A B C Water Testing Apparatus for Paper
Makers. Stencil Plates, &c.

91. Compo-Lithograph Co., The, 161, Weston Street, London, S E.

The "Compo-Lithograph" and Apparatus for reproducing
copies of any written matter, but differing from any
other "Graph," inasmuch as no washing is required,
neither is it necessary to remelt the composition.
Also various compositions for Graph-making Inks and
for using therewith.

92. Ironmonger, T. & Co., The Reliance Hemp and Flax Mills, Wolverhampton.

Twines (Grey, White, Coloured), Laid Cords, &c., suitable for Stationers' and Printers' use; also all descriptions of Twines, Laid Cords, and sundry Lines suitable
for sale by Wholesale and Retail Stationers.

93. EHRMANN, W., Fürth, Bavaria.

Sole Agents for Great Britain: S. WAGNER & Co., 27, Monkwell Street, London, E.C.

Superior Bronze Powders, having the highest brilliancy. and free from fat, manufactured by Mr. Ehrmann's new invention, rendering them far superior to ordinary Bronze Powders. Specially prepared for Lithographers, Paperhanging Manufacturers, &c. Prize Medal Paris Exhibition, 1867; only Prize at the International Exhibition at Berlin, 1878. Branch Establishment at 98, William Street, New York, U.S.A.

94. EYRE & SPOTTISWOODE, Great New Street, London, E.C.

ROW NO. 29.

FROM EAST END TO CENTRE.

95. DORRINGTON, WILLIAM, 2, Charlton Villas, Mayes Road, Wood Green, London, N.

Press News; or, Printers' Trade Magazine. Published Monthly. Price 2d.

96. MARSHALL, T. J. & Co., Gillett Street, Kingsland, London, N., and Invicta Works, 26, Overy Street, Dartford, Kent.

Dandy Rolls, with Patent Watermarking.
Improved Universal Dandy Roll Carriages.
Bank-Note Moulds, Paper Machine Wires.
Pure Red Rubber Deckle Straps.
Vulcanized India Rubber Belting, &c.

97. COATES BROS., Printing Ink and Varnish Manufacturers, 74, Fann Street, London, E.C. ; Works : West Ham.

Case, containing Specimens of Lithographic and Letter-press Inks, Black and Colored, with Printings of same, Bronze Powders, Lithographic Letter-press Varnishes, Fine Colours, &c.

98. BROWN, BENJAMIN GEORGE & Co., 44, Collingwood Street, Blackfriars Road, London, S.E.

Machine Oiler	...	No. 0.—Price 12s 0d per doz.
Ditto	...	,, 1 ,, 14s 6d ,,
Ditto	...	,, 2 ,, 20s 0d ,,
Ditto	...	,, 3 ,, 24s 6d ,,
Ditto	...	,, 4 ,, 27s 0d ,,

Needle Lubricators, from 6s. per dozen.

99. WEINSCHENK & Co., 7, Grocers' Hall Court, London, E.C.

Bronze Powders, in all Shades, and Leaf Metals.

100. A COLLECTION OF PROVINCIAL NEWSPAPERS, FORWARDED FOR EXHIBITION BY THE PROPRIETORS.

101. WALMESLEY & LEWIS, Fine Art Publishers and Frame Manufacturers, 17, Park Street, Islington, London, N.

Frames, Photographs, Christmas and Birthday Cards (printed and hand-painted).

102. STOTZ & WINTER, 31, Jewin Street, London, E.C.

Fine Colours : blue, pink, and violet. Ultramarines.
Bronze Powders and Leaf Metal.

103. MASTER, JOHN, 175, Goswell Road, London.

Brushes of every description for printers, bookbinders, stationers, electro- and stereotypers, gilders, silversmiths, metal-polishers, &c.

104. GUTTENBURG WOOD TYPE COMPANY, LIMITED, The, Geneva, Switzerland.

London Agent : M. J. BOISSON, 89, Charlotte Street, Fitzroy Square, W.C.

Samples of Wood Type.
Samples of Zinc Plates.

105. PAUL, J. C., Granville Place, King's Cross Road, London, W.C.

Type Cases and Printers' Joinery.

106. MORTON, CHARLES, 167, City Road, London, E.C.

Type-casting Machines in operation.
Type in Founts.
Specimens.

107. UNWIN BROS., 109A, Cannon Street, London, E.C.

Specimens of Photo-Lithography, Chromo-Lithography.
Specimens of Photo-Lithography and Letter-press Printing.
Lowell's Steel Plate Cards.
Enamelled Zinc Tablets.
Enamelled Iron Tablets.
Glass Tablets.
" Specialite " Iron Tablets.

108. HEYER & PESTOR, Ingelleim-on-the-Rhine.

Sole Agent: M. L. SPIER, 6, New Street, Bishopsgate Street, London, E.C.

Straw Pulp and Material.

Pommersche Papier Fabrick, Hohenkrug, near Mühlenbeck, in Pommern. *London Agent:* M. L. Spier, 6, New Street, Bishopsgate.
Every description of Packing Papers.

109. Thomson, Sterne & Co., 9, Victoria Chambers, Westminster, London, S.W.; and the Crown Iron Works, Glasgow.

Automatic Knife-grinding Machines for sharpening chisel-edged knives up to 60 inches in length. These machines are constructed to grind automatically plane irons, paper cutting knives, curriers' knives and all others having chisel edges.

These machines carry a consolidated emery wheel, 20 inches in diameter by 1½ inches broad, the spindle of which runs at 270 revolution per minute and is fitted with fast and loose pulleys, 7¾ inches diameter by 3 inches broad, with belt shifter complete.

The table carrying the knives to be ground has a self-acting motion, from side to side, in front of the emery wheel, and can be set to any traverse required.

Water is supplied to the emery wheel, which preserves the temper of the knives when being ground, and these can be set to any required bevel of chisel edge, and are fed towards the emery wheel by the small hand wheels, at either end of the machine.

These machines are easily set up, and require no foundation, except fixing to the floor; and as they automatically grind the knives perfectly straight, and with a true bevel edge, they will be found very valuable to all parties using long knives with chisel edges.

110. Dettelbach, R., 34, Camomile Street, London, E.C. *Sole Agent* for T. Rosenfels, Fürth, Bavaria.

Gold and Silver Papers.
Borders and Ornaments, in Gold, Silver, Ivory, Velvet, and various fancy papers.

111. STONHILL, W. J., 5, Ludgate Circus Buildings, London, E.C.

Current and Back Numbers of the *British and Colonial Printer, Stationer, and Paper Trade Review*, published on the 1st and 16th of each month, at 5, Ludgate Circus Buildings, London, E.C. : W. J. Stonhill, proprietor. Subscriptions, 8/- per annum.

Specimen copies of the Trade Journals of America, the Continent, and the Colonies.

Samples of fibres showing progress from raw state to a sheet of paper.

ROW NO. 30.

FROM EAST END TO CENTRE.

112. MARR TYPE FOUNDING Co., LIMITED, The, Whiteford House, Edinburgh, and 19, Charterhouse Street, London, E.C.

Printing Types, Cases, Frames, Rules, and other articles used by Letter-press Printers.

113. LAWRENCE BROS., Viaduct Works, Farringdon Road, London, E.C.

American Specialities, viz., The Eagle Pencil Company's Cedar Pencils, Copyable Pencils, Solid Ink Pens, &c.

McLoughlin Bros.' Games, Picture Books, &c.

The New York Consolidated Card Company's Playing Cards, and a full line of Stationers' Sundries all of American origin.

114. DURABLE PRINTERS' ROLLER COMPANY, LIMITED, The, Viaduct Works, Farringdon Road, London, E.C.

"The Durable" Compo and Rollers for Letter-press Printing Machines.

The "Ultimatum" India Rubber Rollers for Litho' and Letter-press Printing.

Specimens of the W. H. Page Wood Type.

Specimens of American Printing Ink—Gloss and Brilliant Black.

Specimens of Sensitive Ink for Cheque and Copyable Commercial Printing.

115. SHELDON, ALFRED, Millwright and Engineer, Wells, Somerset.

Machine specially designed for Sharpening and Grooving Brass Rag Engine Plates, manufactured by the Exhibitor; also Brass Engine Plates, Grooved Special Bearings for Hot Cylinders for Paper Machines, Mill Gearing, Wheels, Pulleys, &c.

An assortment of Hydraulic, Steam Vacuum, and Water Gauges, Engine Counter and Steam Fittings.

116. COOKE, HENRY & Co., Paper Manufacturers, Richmond, Yorkshire.

Model of New and Improved Rag Engine for Washing, Beating, and Bleaching various kinds of Paper Makers' Material. (In use.)

Model of Air Diffusing Fire Bar. (In use.)

Drawings of Improved Turbine, adapted for high and low falls.

117. CROOKES, ROBERTS & Co., Argus Works, Sheffield.

Engine Plates, Roller Bars, Millboard Knives, Chopper Knives, Paper Knives, Circular Cutters, and other Tools used by Paper Makers.

N

118. DONKIN, BRYAN & Co., Engineers, 55A, South-wark Park Road, Bermondsey, London, S.E.

Machine for Sharpening the Steel Roll Bars and Plates of Rag Engines, without taking the Plates to pieces, or removing the Rolls from their position in the Rag Engines, thus ensuring greater accuracy and uniformity in cutting, besides saving much time and trouble as compared with the old style of cutting by hand. To plane the Roll Bars, it is only necessary to unbolt the top part of the Machine which holds the tool, and lay it across the Rag Engine Trough in front of the Roll. The Machine as here exhibited is for Planing the Plates; it can be had for driving either by hand or power.

Drawings of the first Printing Machine, invented and made in 1814 by the Exhibitors.

119. GREEN, G. F. & Co., 3, George Yard, Lombard Street, London, E.C.

Special Exhibits:—

Unbleached Chemical Wood Pulp, manufactured at Delary Mill by the Malmö Trämassefabriks Aktie Bolag, Malmö (Sweden), with specimens of the wood in different stages of manufacture, and samples of the recovered soda produced by a special process.

Bleached and Unbleached Chemical Wood Pulp, manufactured by the Danziger Cellulose Fabrik, Danzig, with specimens of wood in the different stages of manufacture.

General Exhibits:—

Chemical Wood and Straw Pulps (bleached and un-bleached), Pine and Aspen Pulps, Wood Flour, Wood Pulp Middle Cuttings, Wood Pulp Boards, Wood Pulp Middles, "Patent" Brown Wood Pulp Boards, manu-factured in Sweden, Norway, Holland, Belgium, Finland, Germany, and other countries. G. F. GREEN & Co., *Sole Agents* for these Mills in the United Kingdom.

120. STURROCK, JOHN & SON, Engineers' Brass-founders, Manderston Foundry, 91, Leith Walk, Leith.

Anderson's Patent Wire Guide.

Bruce's Patent Wire Guide.

Improved Patent Wire Guide.

Improved Steam Cock and Knee for Drying Cylinders.

Gland Cock and Knee and Gland for Drying Cylinders.

Improved Safety Valve.

121. WATSON, HENRY & SON, High Bridge Works, Newcastle-on-Tyne.

Flat Jogging Strainer Frame with old strainer plates, formerly worn to cut No. 5, renovated and closed to cut No. 3.

122. LETTS, SON & CO., LIMITED, 33, King William Street, E.C., and North Road, New Cross, London, S.E.

Time-saving Publications.

Account Books.

Atlases and Geographical Works.

Stationery Sundries.

Colour Printing, &c. &c.

123. STONHILL, W. J., 5, Ludgate Circus Buildings, London, E.C.

ROW No. 31.

FROM CENTRE END TO WEST END.

124. RICHMOND, JOSEPH & Co., 31, Kirby Street, Hatton Garden, London, E.C.

BOOKBINDING MACHINERY.—

Steam Power Blocking and Inking Press, "Richmond's Patent."

Steam Power Blocking and Inking Press, " Gough's Patent."

Guillotine Cutting Machine (31-in. steam or hand power).

Pair of 6-in. Hydraulic Presses, with Pump.

Millboard Cutting Machine, for steam power.

Circular Saw Bench, for Bookbinders' use.

Imperial Blocking Press, No. 1 size.

Ditto   ditto   No. 2 size.

Backing Machine, 12-in.

Trimming Machine (steam power), for Magazine Work.

STATIONERS' MACHINERY.—

Envelope Folding Machine (steam power), " Reay's Patent."

Envelope (Lever) Cutting Machine.

Relief Colour Stamping Press, " Gough's Patent," with Automatic Colouring and Wiping-off arrangement.

Cameo Colour Stamping Press, " Gough's Patent," Self Colouring.

Guillotine Cutting Machine, 31-in. (steam or hand power).

Pair of 6-in. Hydraulic Presses, with Pump.

Folding Machine, for Quire Work.

Envelope Cutters.

Printers' Machinery.

Guillotine Cutting Machine, 31-in. (steam or hand power).

Pair 6-in. Hydraulic Presses, with Pump.

Hydraulic Press and Pump, for Electrotyping purposes.

125. Crown Steam Printing Company, The, Crown Court, Milton Street, Fore Street, London, E.C. (W. O. Waud, Manager).

Specialities for Printers :—

Specimen-books for the Trade.

Almanacs and Calendars.

Fancy Bordered Cards.

Ball Programmes.

The " Triform " Cards.

Menu Cards.

Floral Borders.

Oxford Border Flat Tints.

The " Esthetic " Cards.

Specimens of General Printing.

Do.   Photo-Lithography.

Do.   Mechanical Reductions.

Do.   Engraving.

Do.   Black and White Reverses.

Do.   Litho-Electro Surface Blocks.

Luminous Faces, Balmain's Patent ⎫   Sole

Magic Watch-boxes,   ditto.   ⎭ Manufacturers.

See Advertisement (Page 51).

126. Doubble, Thomas, Bartlett's Buildings, and King's Head Court, Holborn, London.

Slates. These Slates have a piece of wire let into a groove that runs round the edge of the frame. This wire is secured, and effectually prevents the frame from coming to pieces. The slates are manufactured by machinery, and so carefully put together as not to rattle when in use. They are also made in boo shape, &c.

127. DEAN & SON, Publishers, &c., 160A, Fleet Street, London, E.C.

The "Stationer" Fancy Trades Register.
Toy Books.
Christmas Cards.
Packets of Chromo-printed Texts, Mottoes.
Relief and other Scraps, and Scrap-books.
New Style Flower-pot Covers, and other Fancy Goods.

128. SMITH & WOLFF, 5, Falcon Street, Aldersgate Street, London, E.C.

Specimens of Vellum Binding and Account Books.

129. WOLFF, E. & SON, 55, Great Queen Street, Holborn, W.C., and Falcon Pencil Works, Battersea, London, S.W.

Black Lead Pencils, Crayons, Indelible Ink Pencils.

Drawing Materials and Stationery Novelties.

Specialities : Spanish Graphite Pencils, Paper Cleaners, Leads for Ever-pointed Pencils, Indelible Black and Coloured Pencils, Audascript Pens, the Limnoscope or Drawing Apparatus, Eclipse Marking Ink requiring no heating, &c.

At Bay No. 9, see processes in connection with the Manufacture of Black Lead Pencils.

130. ZUCCATO & WOLFF, 15, Charterhouse Street, Holborn Viaduct, London, E.C.

Trypograph, "Zuccato's Patent," a Mechanical System of Printing in indelible black. Proof produced immediately after completion of copy without any preparation, a stencil may be used for reproduction many times, one writing will yield over 5,000 copies, all equally good. In printing the surface of paper is not injured and does not curl up. Process reliable, simple, cleanly and rapid, may be profitably used by Printers executing small jobs required hurriedly and cheaply. Materials not affected by climatic influence. Price from 31/6. Gold Medal, Paris. 1st Degree of Merit, Sydney.

131. MOORE, C. F. (late SCOTT, WATSON, & MEAKINS,) 25, Tysoe Street, Clerkenwell, London, W.C.

Brass Rules, Plain and Ornamental.
Fancy Dashes, &c.,
Ovals and Circles, on solid brass bodies.
Brass Shapes, &c.
Solid Brass Galleys.
The Improved Brass-bound Table Galley.
Mahogany Galleys, with Zinc and Brass bottoms.
Composing Sticks, various.

132. HILDESHEIMER & Co., 15, Silk Street, Whitecross Street, London, E.C.

Framed and Unframed Specimens of Colour Printing in Chromo-Lithography, Oleographs, &c.
Framed and Unframed Specimens of Christmas, New Year, Birthday, and Valentine Cards, Reliefs, Box Prints, &c., &c.

133. CAMERON & FERGUSON, 13, Stationers' Hall Court, London, and at Glasgow.

Account Books.
Envelopes.
Writing and Account Book Papers.
Printing Papers, White, Toned, Coloured, for News, Book, Magazine, and general purposes.
Stationery Sundries, various.

134. BOND, M. A. (now HICKISSON), 75 and 84, South-gate Road, London, N.

M. A. Bond's (now Hickisson) Crystal Palace Gold Medal Marking Ink.

Crystal Palace Marking Ink Pedestal, with Ink, Pen, and Linen Stretcher.

Glass Case, with Framed Linen Specimens, New Transparent Boxes (forming show card,) &c.

135. HINDLEY, E. J., Bourton, Dorset.

One-Horse Power Vertical Steam Engine, complete, on Water-Heater Foundation Tank, requiring no Firing, Price £39.

One-and-a-Half-Horse Power Vertical Steam Engine, on Water-Heater Foundation Tank, requiring no firing, £47.

Six-Horse Power Horizontal Steam Engine. £45.

No. 1 Band and Circular Saw Bench, with Boring Apparatus.

ROW No. 32.

CENTRE END TO WEST END.

136. RICHMOND, J. & Co., 31, Kirby Street, Hatton Garden, London, E.C.

137. CROWN STEAM PRINTING Co., The, Crown Court, Milton Street, London, E.C.

138. DOUBBLE, T., Bartlett's Buildings, and King's Head Court, Holborn, London, E.C.

139. MÜLLER, UHLICH & Co., 37, King William Street, London, E.C.

Centrifugal Drying Machine.
Leather Belting, &c.

140. ROWNEY, J., 58, City Road, London, E.C.

Writings and Printings, Browns and Drabs, Small Hands, Surface Coloured, and Marble Papers.

Straw Boards lined and unlined.

Wood Pulp Boards, lined and unlined.
Coloured Pulp Printings.
Middles and Millboards.

141. WHITEHEAD, MORRIS & LOWE, 167, Fenchurch Street, London, E.C.

Stout Buff Copying Paper, Books, and Sundries.

142. MENUEL, EUGENE, 19, Tysoe Street, London, W.C.

Cast Brass Type.
Brass and Zinc Bottom Galleys.
Cast and Wrought Iron Chases.
Patent Locking-up Apparatus.
Shooting and Composing Sticks.
Hand Paying Machines.
Perforating Machine, &c.

143. STRAKER, S. & SONS, Avenue Works, Bishopsgate Avenue, London, E.C.

Specimens of a New Process of Photo-Lithography, by means of which Photographs of Views, Portraits, Manufacturers' and other Patterns, &c., *from Nature*, are transferred to and printed from Stone and Zinc Plates, enabling a very large reduction to be made in cost, and ensuring absolute fidelity.

144. PHILIPP BROTHERS, 4 & 5, Silk Street, Cripplegate, London, E.C.

Chromo and Lithographic Work, and Fancy Stationery in Crystal Goods, &c.

145. CUMMING, J. B., 79, Great Tower Street, London, E.C.

Hide Cuttings, prepared for Sizing Writing Paper and Paper Hanging Manufacturers.
Glues and Gelatines for Paper Hanging Manufacturers.
Bookbinders' and Printers' Rollers.

146. WALKER, A. E., 24, Bunhill Row, London, E.C.

Parkin's Patent Transfer. Sheets.

School Slates (American).

147. VICKERY, W., 21, Lloyd's Row, St. John Street, Clerkenwell, London.

Ruling Machine Pens and Slides.

Bookbinders' Press and Plough.

Stabbing Machine and Graining Boards.

148. TROUGHTON, RICHARD, Hermes Street, Pentonville, London, N.

Improved Upper School or College Desk.

Plain Desk with Shelf under, with separate seats to turn up.

Iron Elbow Desk, forming Backed Seat or Table.

School-Board Desk.

Single Desk, with Reading Slope and Frame at back for Copy.

Single Locker Desk, not requiring to be fixed to floor.

Improved Single Desk and Seat combined; the back of desk forming the seat, back of desk in front to economise space.

149. SEEKINGS, J. J. & Co., Quay Street Ironworks, Gloucester.

Three-horse-power Steam Engine combined, with Horizontal Multitubular Boiler, having Cylindrical Firebox surrounded by water, and every part most easy of access.

150. LINFORD, C. & Co., Leicester Gas Motor Works, Leicester.

The "Leicester Gas Motor"—the only Gas Engine at present in the market wherein the motive power is balanced upon the Crank Shaft. No foundations are required; first cost covers all. The consumption of Gas is less than One Penny per hour per horse power.

151. GENERAL ENGINE AND BOILER COMPANY, The, Hatcham Iron Works, Pomeroy Street, New Cross Road, London, S.E.

Eight Nominal Horse-power Patent Horizontal Engine, with Automatic Variable Expansion Gear, Steam Jacketed Cylinder, with Governor, Stop Valve and Independent Foundation Stands. Price £100.

Twelve Nominal Horse-power Patent Horizontal "Express" Engine, with Governor, Feed Pump and Stop Valve, and on Cast Iron Stands. Price, with Pulley, £59 10s.

One Horse-power Engine, with Gas-heated Boiler. Including Feed Pump, price £42.

Fifteen Horse-power Patent Feed Water Heater. Price £10.

ROW NO. 33.

CENTRE END TO WEST END.

152. GOODALL, C. & Sons, Camden Works, London, N.W.

Playing Cards, Mounting Boards, Card Boards, Printing Cards, Ivory Cards and Boards, Note-papers, Envelopes in Boxes, Christmas Cards, Ball Programme and Menu Cards.

Samples of Chromo-Lithographic Printing for Illustrations, &c.

PATENT PRINTING SURFACE COMPANY, The, 281, Strand, London; and Paris. Inventors and Sole Patentees of Rubber Stamps.

Patent Polygonal Stamps, useful as Pocket Self-Inkers or Pad Stamps.

The "Multum" Three and Four Facet in Nickel Silver.

The " Universal " Facet and Dater.

The " Blocklet " ditto Initialer and Numberer.

" Pencil " and " Pocket Facet," " Dauphin " Monogram Dove, &c.

Pad Stamps, Raw and Manufactured Rubber, &c., &c. Protected at home and abroad under Leighton's Patents. Three Awards, Paris, 1878, for the Invention of Rubber Surfaces. Their application to appliances for Printers.

153. LONDOS & Co., Japanese and Chinese Importers, 126 & 127, London Wall, London, E.C.

Samples of Japanese and Chinese Papers, suitable for Box-makers, Bookbinders, Printers, Engravers, Bag-makers, Decorators, &c.

154. CONISBEE, W., & SON, 40, Herbert's Buildings, Waterloo Road, London, S.E.

Double Demy Anglo-French Lithographic Machine.

Demy Folio Wimbledon Cylinder Machine.

26-in. Vertical and Diagonal Paper Cutting Machine.

Foolscap Folio Atlas Treadle Platen Machine.

Samples of First Class Roller Moulds.

Specimens of Material used in founding the same, and tools used therein.

155. LATHAM BROS., Ridgway Gates, Bolton, Lanca-shire.

Patent Rotary Round Hole Perforator, for making round hole perforations, as in postage stamps, with one line of perforation or a number of lines simultaneously, allowing the perforation to be stopped at any distance, sheets fed in 4 or 5 together.

Trimming Machine for Cutting Books or Magazines where the fold in the section is required to be left uncut.

Stabbing Machine for Book Sewing.

156. COHEN, B. S., 24, Great Prescot Street, London, E.

Pencils and processes connected with Pencil-making.

157. NICHOLSON, JOHN & SONS, 59 Well Street, Bradford, Yorkshire.

Three-quarter Portrait of Her Majesty the Queen.

Portraits of the Duke and Duchess of Edinburgh, surrounded with groups of flowers.

Chromo Calendar, emblematical of the birth of the New Year.

Emblem of the Typographical Society, illustrative of the rise and progress of the Typographical art.

Set of Chromo-Lithos (subjects for tradesmen's Presentation Calendars—"Buttercups and Daisies," "Under the British Flag," "The Deserter," "Nearer My God to Thee," "Simply to Thy Cross I cling," "Italian Beauty," "Swiss Girl," "Neapolitan Girl."

158. CLARK, THACKRAY & Co., Newlay, near Leeds.

Glues and Gelatines, made entirely from the roundings and fleshings from hides, calf and sheep skins. Suitable for bookbinders, pianoforte makers, billiard table makers, match makers, emery cloth makers, and any other description of work where glue is an essential.

159. LAW, SONS & Co., Windsor Court, Monkwell Street, London. E.C.,

Bookbinders' Cloth.

Gold and Silver Cloth, suitable for scrap books, music cases, and other fancy bindings.

160. CAMPBELL, DUNCAN & SON, 96 St. Vincent Street, Glasgow.

Campbell's Diaries, published at Glasgow.

161. HAYDEN, W. H. & Co., 10, Warwick Square, Paternoster Row, E.C., London, *Sole Agents for England.*

Bewly & Draper's Ink Dichroic.

Black Writing Ink in bottles, quarts, pints and half-pints.

Specimen bottles for distribution to the trade.

162. HAWTIN, WILLIAM & SON, 24 & 25, Paternoster Row, London, E.C.

Samples of Account Books with improved Spring Backs, giving greater strength and more lasting elasticity in the opening of the book, and increased facility to the writer when approaching the pence or other columns where folded.

163. MARX, MARCUS, 11, Wansey Street, Walworth, London, S.E.

Type and Stencil Plates for Marking Linen, Books, &c., also Pens for Writing without Ink.

163A. TURNER, H. J., 28, High Street, Birmingham.

Specimens of Enamelled Iron.

Enamelled Iron Show Tablets, &c.

Litho-Printing on Iron in all sizes and colors, designed specially for the trade.

164. GUY, JOHN & SONS, 1A & 2B, Hoxton Street, London, N.

Stationery Cabinets.

Inkstands.

Copying Presses and Stands.

Office and Counting-house Furniture.

Stationers' Sundries.

ROW NO. 34.

CENTRE TO WEST END.

165. GOODALL, C. & SON, Camden Works, London, N.W.

166. SPELLER & PRESTON, 19, Finsbury Street, London, E.C.

Manufactured Stationery.

167. CONISBEE, W. & SON, 40, Herbert Buildings, Waterloo Road, London, S.E.

168. DANIELL, S. A., Edward Street, Parade, Birmingham.

Copying Presses, various qualities.

169. KING, SON & WHITAKER, 4 & 5, Old Bailey, London, E.C.

Note Paper in fancy wrappers, 1s. Boxes of Note Paper and Envelopes.

Account Books in various bindings.

Manuscript Books, and General Stationery.

170. ARMITAGE & IBBETSON, Chromo-Lithographers, Bradford, Yorkshire

Specimens of the various kinds of work executed by Exhibitors in Chromos, Show Cards, Labels, Embossed Work, and Engraving.

171. Ford, T. B., Snakeley Paper Mill, Loudwater, High Wycombe.

Glass Case containing Sample Sheets of the superior 428 Mill White and Coloured Blottings, with a Blotting Case attached, also containing Sample Sheets. *Varieties*: White, Pink, Deep Pink, Buff, Blue, Mauve, and Antique Mauve, of which latter Exhibitor is the original maker, and introducer of the name. Well-known qualities, open and absorbent, pleasant softness of feel in using, moderately strong and durable, not soon fraying to pieces, being made of good material, not liable to become hard and close or lose colour by keeping, and well adapted for exportation. Mills now employed in manufacturing 428, 429, and 509. Established 1880. N.B.—A Prize Medal Label and 428 Mill on each ream.

172. Hamer, W., · British Empire Chambers, 71, Market Street, Manchester.

Chemically Prepared Wood Pulp, manufactured by the Hafslunds Chem Træmassefabrik, Hafslund Chemical Wood Pulp Co., Sarpsborg, Norway.

Mechanically Prepared Wood Pulp (Pine and Aspen), manufactured by Mr. P. Anker, Frederikshald, Norway. *Sole Agent for United Kingdom*, W. Hamer.

173. Lehmann & Sankey, Westphalia Mills, Bow.

Millboard, various qualities.

Strawboard, various qualities.

Middles.

Tough Glazed and Unglazed Packing Papers.

Patent Asphalte Paper Roofing.

174. Lotz, W. T. & Co., 20, Barbican, London, E.C.

McGill's Single-stroke Staple Presses for inserting paper-fasteners, and for binding pamphlets.

Paper-fasteners.

Suspending-rings, &c.

175. STIDSTONE, C. W., 23, Moorgate Street, London, E.C.

High Class Hand-painted Christmas and New Year Cards.

Specialities on Silk and Ivory.

Account-books that can be relied upon for hard wear, and showing careful attention to details.

176. CITY RUBBER STAMP Co., The, 4, Newgate Street, E.C. E. M. RICHFORD, *Manager.*

Rubber Endorsement Stamps of every description.

Specialities in Rubber Monograms, Initials, Designs, Trade Marks, &c.

Solid Rubber Type for Hand-printing.

Specimens of Inks.

Printing Press for printing hand-bills, &c. from Rubber Dies.

Dating Stamps and Machines, &c.

177. HAMMOND, DAVY, 259 & 264, Hackney Road, London, E.

Patent Slates and Slate-ruling Machine, with samples of cheap Bookbinding.

178. HILL & Co., 48 Essex Street, Strand, London, W.C.

Specimens of Engraving on Wood, &c.

179. DEFRIES, N. & Co., 18, 19 & 20, Barbican, London, E.C.

Cloth Labels, Printing, &c.

180. GUY, J. & SONS, 1A. and 2B, Hoxton Street, London, N.

ROW NO. 35.

CENTRE TO WEST END.

181. TAYLOR, W. G. & Co., 14, Little Tower Street, London.

Esparto, Wood Pulp, Jute, and sundry fibres.
Foreign Rags, &c.
Caustic Soda, Soda Ash, Crystal Soda.
Alum, Refined Alkali, Bleaching Powder, &c.
Rosin, China Clay, Starch, Farina, &c.

182. RICHARDSON, NICHOLAS GOSSELIN, Tyaquin, Athenry, Co. Galway.

Specimens of "Purple Melic Grass," "Molina Corulla," collected off the deep red bogs at Tyaquin, County Galway; some of the Paper Millboards are made solely of this Grass, by Mr. William Smith, Golden Bridge Paper Mill, Dublin, and others consist of the Grass mixed with other materials.

183. LLOYD, E., Lloyd's Paper Mills, Sittingbourne, Kent.

News, in reels, as made for printing *Lloyd's News* and *The Daily Chronicle.*

Samples, showing the various changes from Raw Material to Paper.

184. DUPUY, TH. & SON, 120 & 121, Newgate Street, London, E.C.

Specimens of work in Chromo-Lithography and Colour Printing, Oleographs, Christmas Cards, Transfers and Showcards.

" The Princess," Dupuy's Magazine of Fashion, Literature and Art; and " Santa Claus," Dupuy's Christmas Annual.

Patent Paper Panels, for Artists or Carriage Builders.

185. FABER, A. W., 149, Queen Victoria Street, London, E.C.

Lead and Coloured Pencils.

Artists' Materials.

General Stationery.

186. KONIG, OTTO & Co., 15, Cross Street, Finsbury Place, London, E.C.

Alois Dessauer, of Aschaffenburg, exhibits all classes of Fancy Papers.

Leo Haenle, of Munich, exhibits all classes of Gold and Silver Papers, Borders, and Bronze Powders.

Dr. C. Leverkus & Sons, of Leverkusen, near Cologne, exhibits Ultramarine Blues.

Agent : Otto Konig, 15, Cross Street, Finsbury, E.C.

187. ERHARDT, H. & Co., 9, Bond Court, Walbrook, London, E.C.

Vegetable Parchment for Writing, Printing, Packing, and for Tying over Jars, Bottles, &c.

Tinfoil in any Thickness up to 14,000 square inches to the lb., also Coloured and Gold Foil.

188. SULMAN, BENJAMIN, Metropolitan Works, 63 & 64, Milton Street, Fore Street, London, E.C.

Die Sinking.

Official Seal Engraving.

Relief Stamping.

Illuminating.

Pure Rubber Stamps.

Screw, Embossing, Copying, Lever, and Perforating Presses.

Christmas and New Year Cards.

Valentines.

Fancy Stationery, &c.

189. MORDAN, S. & Co., 41, City Road, London, E.C.

Gold, Silver, Ivory, and Porcupine Quill Pencil Cases.

Cedar Pencils and Patent Leads.

Silver and Ivory Penholders.

Plain and Fancy Postage Scales.

Deed and Cash Boxes.

Fire and Thief-proof Safes.

Copying Presses, Screw and Portable.

Seal Presses, Screw and Lever.

Perforating and Eyeleting Presses.

Patent Bramah Locks.

Gold and Silver Smelling Bottles and Silver Card Cases.

Memorandum and Menu Tablets, &c.

190. LUKS, WILLIAM, 14, Bedford Street, Covent Garden, London.

Floral Hand-painted Birthday Cards, Christmas Cards and Wedding Cards.

Photographs of Celebrities in Cabinet size and Carte size, both plain and coloured.

Photographs framed in Carved Wood Frames, Brass Frames, and other Frames.

Also other Fine Art Publications.

191. HICKS, W. S., 45, St. Mary Axe, London, E.C.

American Pocket Pencil Cases.

Toothpicks and Gold Pens, and Novelties of the finest quality and workmanship, made at exhibitor's own manufactory in New York.

192. SCHROEDER, F. & Co., 14, Charterhouse Buildings, London, E.C.

Straw Boards, lined and unlined Binders' Boards.

Wood Pulp Boards and Millboards.

Printing Papers.

Fancy Papers, coloured, flint glazed and enamelled, plain and embossed.

Morocco Marble Gelatine Papers.

Gold and Silver Papers.

193. ROBEY & Co., Engineers, Lincoln.

One 4-horse Power Single Cylinder Patent " Robey " fixed Engine and Locomotive Boiler combined.

One 2-horse Power Improved Vertical Engine and Patent Tubulous Boiler combined.

One 4-horse Power Single Cylinder Horizontal fixed Steam Engine of the most improved design.

ROW NO. 36.

CENTRE TO WEST END.

194. CAMERON, AMBERG & Co., Manufacturers and Patentees, 70, Queen Street, London, E.C.

Amberg's Letter Filing Devices.

Foster's " Premium " File.

These articles are well and handsomely made, and of the greatest assistance in keeping miscellaneous papers and correspondence in the best of order with the least trouble, and in matter of reference are simply invaluable·

195. Cropper, H. S. & Co., Minerva Works, Nottingham.

Patent Oxy-Hydro. Gas Engine.

Patent Minerva Platen Printing Machines, Foolscap Folio and Demy Folio.

196. Engelbert & Co., 70 & 71, Bishopsgate Street, London, E.C.

"Engelbert's Lubricator," a First Class Lubricant, absolutely non-corrosive and specially suitable for Cylinders, Shafting, Heavy Bearings, Hot Rollers, &c., as it is non-volatile at 600° F.

197. Zorn, Bahnson, & Co., 9 and 11, Garrick Street, Covent Garden, London, W.C.

Grey and Yellow Lithographic Stones.

Lithographic Writers' and Draughtsmen's Utensils, and Printing Requisites.

Engraving Machines and Utensils.

Bronze Powders.

Fine Dry Colours for Lithographic and Typographical Printing.

Lithographic and Lettor-press Printing-inks.

198. Toiray, G., 238, Blackfriars Road, London, S.E.

Inks, Writing and Copying.

199. Wyman & Sons, 74 and 75, Great Queen Street, London, W.C.

Printing Times and Lithographer.

Wcrks relating to Printing and allied trades.

200. ZUMBECK, AUG. & Co., 21, Mincing Lane, London, E.C.

Wood Pulp, Moist and Dry.

Pine and Aspen Paste.

Blue Aniline Colours.

Nitrate of Lead.

Sugar of Lead.

Aluminous Cake.

Alum.

201. BAILEY, W. H. & Co., Albion Works, Salford, Manchester.

Lehmann's Hot Air Engine. For all purposes this Engine is the cheapest description of applied power; has no Boiler, no fear of explosion, is self-contained, and will work with any kind of ,fuel—such as Peat, Spent Bark, &c. The waste heat can be used for heating room.

202. BATTLEY & Co., Edith Street, Great Cambridge Street, Hackney Road, London, E.

Samples of Vegetable and Spirit Blacks for Printing Inks.

203. GREY & MARTEN, Southwark Bridge, London, S.E.

Improved Composition Cutting Plates and Bars for Envelope Makers and others.

Antimonial Lead and Alloys of Antimony, Tin, and Lead for Typefounders.

204. MORDAN, S. & Co., 41, City Road, London, E.C.

205. CASLON, H. W. & Co., Type Founders, 22 & 23, Chiswell Street, London, E.C.

Printing Type.

Specimen of Printing Types.

Patent Locking Apparatus.

206. THEYER & HARDTMUTH, Vienna. *Agent:* F. STÖTZER, 7, Bull and Mouth Street, London, E.C.

Specimens of Die Sinking, Illuminating, Litho' Printing of Cards, Paper, and Envelopes.

Speciality—High class Illuminated Writing Papers in Fancy Boxes.

207. BRADBURY, WILKINSON & Co., Farringdon Road, London, E.C.

Bunyard's Patent Self-supporting Portfolios.

Bunyard's Patent Easel Portfolios, made of a patent material not liable to warp, and fixed on stands of various kinds of polished woods.

Portrait Albums in various sizes and bindings, plain, and with floral and other designs, hand-painted and printed

Scrap Albums and Books in Morocco and Cloth.

Artists' Stationery, Sketch Books, Solid Sketch Blocks, Mounting Boards, Cut Mounts, and Drawing Boards.

Portfolios, guarded and plain.

INDEX TO ADVERTISEMENTS.

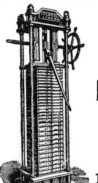

GOLD MEDAL,
PARIS EXHIBITION.

SPOTTISWOODE & CO.,

PRINTERS,

LITHOGRAPHERS, LAW & GENERAL STATIONERS.

Printing Offices:

NEW-STREET SQUARE, FLEET STREET, E.C.

Stationery and Printing:

54, GRACECHURCH STREET, E.C.

Law and General Stationery and Lithography:

87, CHANCERY LANE, W.C.

Parliamentary and Law Stationery and Lithography:

30, PARLIAMENT ST., WESTMINSTER, S.W.

PRINTERS OF

Kew Gardens Official Guides.

South Kensington Museum Official Guide.

Sutton and Son's Illustrated Catalogue.

Heal and Son's Illustrated Catalogue.

New Civil Service Co-operative Price List.

Universities' Co-operative Price List.

City of London Co-operative Price List.

Oxford and Cambridge Toilet Club Price List.

Channel Islands Supply Association's Price List.

Messrs. Henry S. King & Co.'s Price List.

And numerous other Catalogues, Lists and Publications,

Invite attention to the SPECIAL FACILITIES which they possess for this class of business.

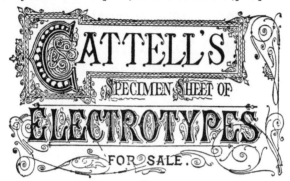

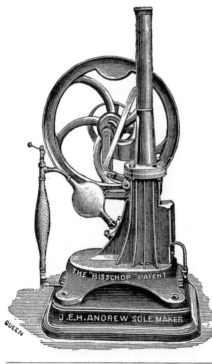

HENRY & LEIGH SLATER,
Warehouse—Dantzic Street, Manchester.

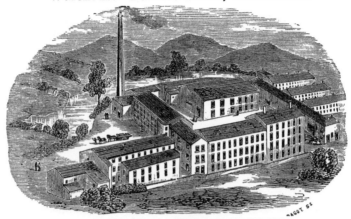

MILL—BOLLINGTON, NEAR MACCLESFIELD.

MANUFACTURERS OF

DULL ENAMELS FOR BEST COLOUR PRINTING.
WHITE AND TINTED ENAMELS.
GLAZED GREEN, BLUE, MAGENTA, &c., for FANCY BOX MAKERS.

Surface Paper for Label Printing, &c. Tin foil Paper. Varnished Paper .Gum Paper.

PATENTEES AND SOLE MANUFACTURERS OF THE CHARTALINE BLANKET.

McGILL'S
PATENT SINGLE-STROKE STAPLE PRESS.

In   } No. 1 for inserting Staples, ¼ & ½ inch & Suspending Rings.
2 Sizes }   „   2   „   „   1, 1½ & 2 inches.

Secured by Royal Letters Patent,
No. 756, 25th Feb., 1879.

For Binding Papers, Pamphlets,
&c., sampling Woollens, Cottons,
Silks, &c., and for suspending
Show Cards. &c., McGill's Patent
Staple Fasteners and Staple Suspending Rings will be found unsurpassed in adaptability. and the
only articles for the purposes
intended that can be applied
automatically. McGill's Patent
Single-Stroke Staple Press auto-
matical·y inserts these Fasteners
and Rings. A single stroke of the
operator's hand upon the Plunger
of the Press will instantaneously
insert and clinch the Staple or
Ring, in the articles to be bound
or suspended.

Staple Suspend-
ing Ring.

ALSO

McGill's Patent American
Paper Fasteners, Binders,
Suspending Rings and
Braces, Picture Hangers,
&c., cheaper and superior
to any other make.

Staple Fastener

Staple Fastener, 2.

EUROPEAN AGENTS—

F. W. LOTZ & Co, 20, Barbican, London, E.C.
Wholesale only. Sold by all Stationers. Exhibited on Stand No. 174.

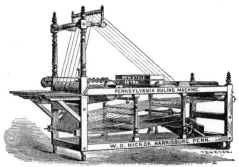

THE BRITISH and COLONIAL Printer & Stationer AND PAPER TRADE REVIEW.

Conducted by - - - - W. JOHN STONHILL.

The Only Journal Devoted to

THE THREE TRADES.

PRINTING	STATIONERY.	PAPER MAKING.
CONTENTS:—	CONTENTS:—	CONTENTS:—
What Printers are Doing.	Technical Articles.	Mill News.
Printing in the Provinces.	Stationery Novelties.	Trade Gossip.
Foreign News.	American Notes.	Sample of Paper.
New Machinery.	Reviews.	Foreign News.
Type Specimens.	Industries of the Trade.	Technical Articles.
Gazette.	Gazette.	Gazette.

Editorial Remarks upon the State of Trade.
Letters from our Correspondents in New York, Canada, and Sydney.
Advertisements of the Principal Firms in the Trade.

PUBLISHED ON
1st and 16th
OF EACH MONTH.

SUBSCRIPTION,
8s. per Ann.,
POST FREE.

Publishing Office:
5, Ludgate Circus Buildings, LONDON, E.C.

N.B.—The above Page is a Sample of Display offered to Advertisers.

THOMAS LONG & CO., Printers' Engineers, EDINBURGH.

ESTABLISHED 1840.

ESTABLISHED 1840.

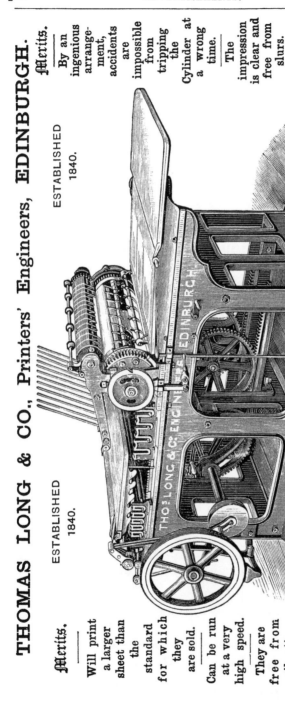

Merits.

Will print a larger sheet than the standard for which they are sold.

Can be run at a very high speed.

They are free from vibration.

They are moderate in price.

Merits.

By an ingenious arrangement, accidents are impossible from tripping the Cylinder at a wrong time.

The impression is clear and free from slurs.

The register is perfect and the distribution faultless.

THE WHARFEDALE MACHINE.

THOMAS LONG & CO. beg to call the attention of Printers, Stationers, and Export Merchants to their improved Wharfedale Machines, which are unsurpassed for simplicity, efficiency, strength, and beauty of design. The workmanship and materials are guaranteed to be of the very best description, and they are offered at a very moderate price. They are in use by many well-known firms, and have given the greatest satisfaction in every case. Price Lists and Testimonials sent to any address upon application. Machines always in stock or progress.

See our Double Demy Machine exhibited in motion on North side of Agricultural Hall, next Messrs. Waterlow and Sons' Limited, stall.

The DIAMOND

Self CLAMP Cutting Machine

(IN USE IN ALL THE LEADING HOUSES)

Will be Worked during the Exhibition

BY

HAZELL, WATSON & VINEY,

6, KIRBY STREET, HATTON GARDEN.

SHUTTLEWORTH & BUNN,

Wholesale Stationers,

COPPER PLATE,

Lithographic and Letter Press Printers,

PAPER BAG MANUFACTURERS, &c.

200, 202, 204 & 206, WATERLOO ROAD,

And 15, 16 & 17, THOMAS STREET, LAMBETH,

LONDON S.E.

**THE TRADE SUPPLIED.—TERMS, PRICES AND SPECIMENS,
POST FREE ON APPLICATION.**

HYATT'S PATENT
WIRE BOUND SCHOOL SLATES

Although of recent introduction, these Slates are generally acknowledged to be decidedly superior to any in the Market ; while others are shaved by hand, these are smoothed by machinery, and thus are of uniform thickness and a perfectly smooth and even surface.

The frame is the lightest as well as the most durable that is made, being secured by a wire passing in a groove entirely round the edge

The writing surface measures the full size for which the Slate is sold, and which size is stamped on frame.

They do not rattle when in use.

The double or counting-house slates are strongly hinged, so as to fold either way.

Prices and all Particulars supplied to the TRADE ONLY by the Sole Agent

THOMAS DOUBBLE,
Manufacturer & Warehouseman,
BARTLETT'S BUILDINGS, LONDON.

SAMPLES ARE EXHIBITED ON GROUND FLOOR.

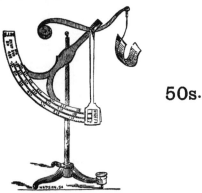

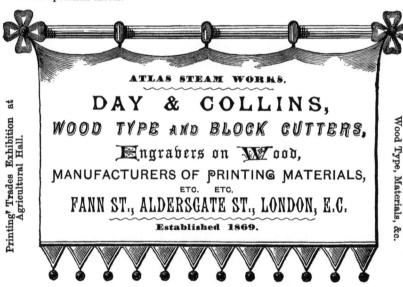

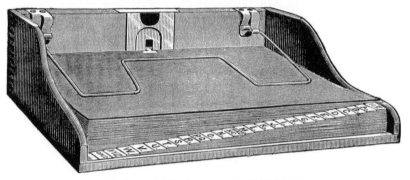

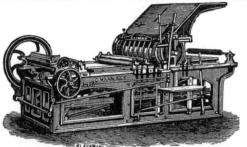
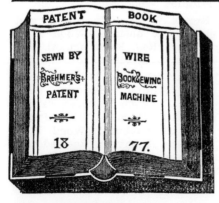

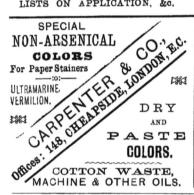

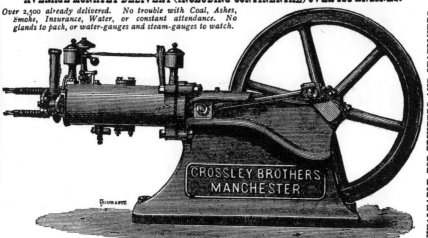